Making Memories That Count

Nurturing Your Child in Christian Values

Debra Fulghum Bruce

CHRISM

02-0345

"The Prize Gift" appeared in a slightly different version in "The Big Ticket Item," *Guideposts Magazine.* Copyright 1993 by Guideposts Associates, Inc., Carmel, N.Y. Used by permission.

Some of the rest of the material in this book also appeared first in article form in various publications.

All Scripture quotations, unless otherwise indicated, are taken from the HOLY BIBLE: NEW INTERNATIONAL VERSION®. NIV®. Copyright © 1973, 1978, 1984 by International Bible Society. Used by permission of Zondervan Publishing House. All rights reserved.

©1994 by Gospel Publishing House, Springfield, Missouri 65802-1894. All rights reserved. No part of this book may be reproduced, stored in a retrieval system, or transmitted in any form or by any means—electronic, mechanical, photocopy, recording, or otherwise—without prior written permission of the copyright owner, except brief quotations used in connection with reviews in magazines or newspapers.

Chrism books are published by Gospel Publishing House.

Library of Congress Catalog Card Number 93-81216
International Standard Book Number 0-88243-345-8
Printed in the United States of America

To my parents, Roy and Jewel Fulghum

Without them, I would have no basis for this book or for my calling as a Christian parent.

Table of Contents

The Key to Meaningful Childhood Memories / 7
  1. Sparks of Faith / 11
  2. "Mommy, Teach Me to Pray" / 15
  3. The Blessing of the Hummingbird / 23
  4. Time Out to Be with God / 27
  5. For Aunt Bub / 32
  6. Be a Storyteller / 36
  7. Adventures in Family Devotions / 41
  8. "Can't I Skip Church?" / 45
  9. When Disappointment Rolls In / 49
10. The Prize Gift / 55
11. Helping Children Share Their Faith / 61
12. When a Morning Lark Marries a Night Owl / 66
13. See the Possibility / 70
14. Correcting the Golden Rule / 74
15. A Guide for Kingdom Living / 77
16. Hope in a Cemetery / 83

17. Not to Worry / 88
18. "My Wife, My Best Friend" / 93
19. Speaking with Sensitivity / 99
20. Respected Children Respect / 105
21. Handling Blue Days / 109
22. Avoiding Manipulation / 114
23. Peacemaker / 119
24. The Power of Touch / 125
25. Giving Up Free Agency / 128
26. Accepting Differences / 132
27. Avoiding Burnout / 138
28. Leave the Label Off / 144
29. Sarah on My Mind / 148
30. How Do You Say It? / 152
31. Liberating the Juggler / 157
32. The Loving Listener / 162
33. Teaching Your Child to Cope / 165
34. Letting Go in Love / 169
35. What Will They Remember? / 174

The Key to Meaningful Childhood Memories

When I finally capture that peaceful moment late at night after my three children are sound asleep, I reflect on the many memories of the day. I laughed to myself one night recently, thinking of the scoop of vanilla ice cream that dropped off young Ashley's cone as she tried to take the first lick. I guess that wouldn't have been so funny except the cold, creamy scoop fell right on her puppy's back. That is not particularly funny either except the puppy squealed and ran through the house and finally tried to rub the ice cream off on my sleeping husband's leg who, in turn, woke up and squealed. Three squealing beings and all for a different reason! A not-so-funny moment actually became a humorous story days later to tell and retell. A memory of childhood was captured in Ashley's mind.

Memory is an interesting phenomenon. There are actually two levels of memory. There is the surface level of memory: the memory of a certain room in your childhood home, the memory of the smell of a particular perfume that your grandmother wore, the memory of the aroma of baking bread, the memory of your grandfather's hands worn rough by years of labor.

All of these are important memories, but they are only on the surface. There is another level of memory: that deep inner reservoir of memory called the subconscious. It is out of our subconscious that come the motivation and power of our lives. From our subconscious come our values and, even more important, our actions.

Solomon spoke about the power of the subconscious: "Above all else, guard your heart, for it is the wellspring of life" (Proverbs 4:23). Jesus said that it is out of the heart that come those things that either make or destroy a person (Luke 6:45).

From this it seems that the subconscious collects information without processing it. That is, what goes into our memories is what comes out. But as parents, we can put together acceptable moments for the memories of our children, of all children. By applying ourselves to this caretaking task, we can create an environment in our homes that will provide our children wholesome, positive memories of their childhood, resulting in a responsible Christian adulthood.

As I look back on my childhood, I have wonderful memories, memories my parents worked diligently to mold. Years before I began my formal education, important lessons such as strong values, a faith in God, social skills, and general rules for getting along in life had been instilled in me by two very important people—my parents.

My memories of childhood reflect my parents holding high the biblical premise that they were ultimately responsible for my actions and reactions as a child; they were my first teachers.

What did they share with me?

1. How to pray and worship God
2. How to be responsible for myself and my belongings
3. How to be a Christian and understand the Bible
4. How to be independent and disciplined
5. How to stand up for what was right and good
6. How to deal with conflict and disappointment
7. How to make wise choices
8. How to respect those in authority and those who are different
9. How to care for others and share with those who have less
10. How to be honest and listen to the ideas of others
11. How to get my priorities in order
12. How to be a committed adult

Now it is my turn to pass along this gift as I nurture my three children—for I feel that parenting is the most important job one can assume. A teacher can leave the students at the end of the day, and her responsibility is basically over. Either the children respond to her teaching by learning or they don't. But a parent's job is never ending; it encompasses every minute of every day with consistent teaching, reprimanding, loving, reasoning, sharing, caring, and more.

Each day we parents have spare moments to teach children what we know about the world. For our children, we, the parents, are the experts in the field of adult living. As parents, we can intentionally choose for our children the kinds of experiences that will help them develop good values, values that will guide them toward acting wholesomely and responsibly in adulthood. On the other hand, we can also unintentionally let negative memories form as we ignore the special times for teaching them. Although we may not feel competent in many areas, as parents we can help our children capture an insight into the real world by giving instruction in daily living.

That is not to say that teaching our children what we know of life means we must sit down with them at age three and begin to cram their crania or drill for a response. Nor does it imply that once our five-year-old can count we should make him add long columns of figures after school. Rather, teaching our children goes beyond providing knowledge; it has to do with giving insight. As parents we have opportunities daily to provide our children with firsthand instruction on how to live in their world.

The Bible affirms this special calling given a parent and emphasizes the need to pass along knowledge to younger generations. The Lord himself instructed the people of Israel so that they in turn would "teach their children" (Deuteronomy 4:10, RSV). Again, in Proverbs 22:6, we are commissioned by Scripture: "Train a child in the way he should go, and when he is old, he will not turn from it."

For us as Christian parents, teaching and training our children in the special attributes of love, caring, and consideration as we have opportunity is important. Yes, the school can instruct in basic social and learning skills, but we must teach the skills of living, such as how to get along with a friend, how to compromise in an argument, how to respect others, how to tolerate differences, how to stand up for righteousness, and how to play fair.

I have taken the liberty to show from my own family's experiences how to turn the activity in a home from a negative to a positive moment, a moment that not only leaves an optimistic impression on the child, but that will return years later as a pleasant childhood memory. Each chapter is filled with true anecdotes, "field-tested" suggestions, and Scripture passages that you can claim for strength and support.

As I wrote *Making Memories that Count,* I prayed daily that it would be a practical parenting guide, demonstrating ways to instill values and responsible social skills in children while creating pleasant memories of childhood for both you and them. So whether you read one chapter or the entire book, you will gain helpful and inspirational material that can assist as you follow the biblical command to "teach your children," making memories that count.

What will our children remember about us? May they say that we loved God, that Christianity was more than just a word to us, that we taught them about living itself. For I believe— and I hope you do too— that all they need to know can come from us, their parents.

1

Sparks of Faith

"Faith comes from hearing the message."

—Romans 10:17

It had been a long, hot summer day. The temperature soared over the ninety degree mark and the humidity in our tropical Florida neighborhood soaked the clothing if any dared to walk outdoors. Our three children reacted, as most children do to uncomfortable conditions, by screaming at each other, name-calling, and an occasional slap or two. And I reacted, as most tired mothers do when the summer vacation seems as if it will never end, by continually reprimanding the children for not getting along.

"Please try to stay out of each other's way," I pleaded with the children. "There is plenty of space in this home for each of you without getting in each other's way."

"But he's on my side of the couch," Ashley screeched as her brother just happened to brush against her skin. "And tell Brittnye to sit down. I can't see the television."

"Well, I can't see either and besides that, I really don't care if you see or not," Brittnye yelled back as she continued to block the view of the other two.

The conversation went on and on and on. My nerves seemed to stand up on my skin as if ready to scream back.

Why do I even try? I wondered silently as I washed the dishes from lunch. I scrubbed the pots harder to try to block out the quarreling coming from the family room.

Then in the midst of the battle sounds the phone rang.

"Take care of Lisa this evening? Of course, bring her right over." Our neighbor had just found out that her mother was being rushed to the emergency room in a diabetic coma and had asked to leave her eight-year-old daughter with us.

After explaining the situation to our three children, I was astonished at the sudden change in dispositions.

"Is she going to be okay, Mom?" my son asked tenderly. "Is she going to die?"

"Oh, poor Lisa," Ashley whimpered. "I know she must feel sad."

"I would be so scared if Grandmommy were taken to the hospital," Brittnye said with empathy in her voice.

Empathy? Tenderness? Right in the midst of the uncontrollable fighting, arguing, and screaming for their own space, these three children suddenly became sensitive, caring, and compassionate young Christians.

What had happened? I like to think this is that special "spark" that comes alive in Christians when there are needs to be met. We go along day after day, routinely functioning in our work or play—until someone is in need. Then we seem to catch ourselves, and even the most routinized among us softens and reaches out and gives.

It does take only a spark to get a fire going. In our family we have seen these sparks of faith brighten even the dullest days. These sparks allow us to realize that our children are truly growing in the Christian faith and can live that selfless love that Jesus taught.

Later that evening when we sat down to dinner, the three warriors had certainly reversed their personalities. As I brought the large platter of spaghetti to the table, I overheard Brittnye telling Lisa of our family traditions.

"Now, every night at dinner we all join hands and have a family prayer," Brittnye said matter-of-factly as she grabbed the hand of the younger child, then took the hand of her brother. "Then we go around the table and pray for someone who needs help."

"Yeah. You can pray for your grandmommy," Ashley chimed in lovingly.

"We all will pray for her grandmother," my oldest son added wisely.

Were these the same three children who had grumbled and

groaned when their father reminded them of our family prayer last night? Were these three actually joining hands in love instead of refusing to touch each other during the usual family prayer?

Again, that special spark of faith came alive! After all these years of praying together, this Christian tradition had become real and important to them, and they wanted to share this comfort with someone who was in need.

I think we can see sparks of faith in our everyday family life, if only we look for them. After all, you must watch a fire closely to see the faintly burning embers among the warm coals. Those tiny embers can be gently fanned to create a warm, glowing fire, just as in our daily lives those tiny sparks of faith can be nurtured in our children to create compassionate Christians.

You can see sparks of faith when you are alone with a child, praying before bedtime. As words are lifted up to the Father in heaven, the child's attention focuses on matters of the heart. You can witness these sparks of faith when a child sings in the choir at church, reads a Scripture verse in Sunday school, or takes a plate of cookies to a neighbor who is ill.

Although you may not see such sparks every day in your children, that does not mean they are not there. As you continue to share your Christian faith with your children, pray and worship as a family, and role model compassionate living, these sparks can flicker brightly in the souls of your young.

A friend shared that she had grown weary from taking her children to church only to hear them fight all the way home in the car.

"Is it worth it?" she asked. "Do you think they even heard the message?"

Yes, I think so. Just as Thomas Edison kept at it until he found the type of filament that would illuminate his electric light bulb, so we must keep at it, teaching and guiding our children until the faith burns steadily in them. We never know when it will begin to glow continuously and brighten fully in maturity.

The Bible teaches us that faith as small as a grain of mustard seed can do enormous tasks. Jesus said, "If you have faith as small as a mustard seed, you can say to this mountain, 'Move from here to there' and it will move. Nothing will be impossible for you" (Matthew 17:20).

Many times as a parent I have felt as if the guidance and inspiration I gave to my children was simply lost. But I have come to believe that all the lessons in Christian discipleship they have been taught as children will come back in their lifetime as they have need to take their faith seriously.

Later that evening when Lisa's mother returned to pick her up, the children were anxiously awaiting the outcome of her grandmother's situation.

"How is your mother?" our oldest son asked quietly. "Is she going to be all right?"

"Well, it was touch and go for a while," my neighbor answered frankly. "But her doctor thinks that as soon as her blood sugar is stable, she should be fine."

Lisa went home to her family relieved that her grandmother would make it through the crisis. And our three children went back into the family room and again began to claim their territory.

"It's my turn to watch my show," Ashley screamed as the older two turned the TV to a movie.

"Get off my pillow," Brittnye said as she yanked her pillow from her brother.

"Mom, I can't stand being near these two," my oldest child complained as the warriors began again.

Yes, the summertime behavior continued. But because of the special sparks that had glowed, I knew that beneath all the bickering and complaining the three were growing in their Christian faith. It was during moments of crises, like our experience with Lisa and her grandmother, that the children leaned on their Christian faith and compassionately witnessed to those in need.

Those special sparks of faith, they are there in your children—Believe me! It may take a crisis or hurtful moment in order for your child to truly express a personal faith, but as you continue to nurture this spark with Christian fellowship, Bible study, and prayer in your home, this spark will glow and warm those around it.

2

"Mommy, Teach Me to Pray"

"The prayer of a righteous man is powerful and effective."
—James 5:16

"Mommy, teach me to pray," Ashley whispered as I tucked her into bed. This innocent request reminded me of the disciples as they asked Jesus for guidance in praying. Just like the disciples, our young daughter desired the intimate Christian experience of talking to God.

Maxie Dunnam describes the human need for prayer, saying, "As living beings, we breathe, we eat, we drink, we sleep. As human beings, we breathe, eat, drink, sleep, and pray. It's a part of our nature as human beings to pray" (*The Workbook of Living Prayer* [Nashville: Upper Room, 1975], 12).

When a child prays, he is communicating with God. A child may not understand the awesome power, but he can experience the comfort and closeness of sharing personal needs with One who cares. Yet a child cannot experience this relationship with the Heavenly Father unless someone takes the time to show him how.

A missionary from overseas stayed in our home recently. During his visit we asked him to say the blessing at our meal. His words were beautifully spoken as he added Scripture verses and meaningful prayer language. One could tell the young man experienced a true personal relationship with God. Yet some of his terms—"thee," "You are the light," and "magnify"—held no meaning for our youngest child.

Praying with children is a delicate matter. What may seem a natural form of communication with our Heavenly Father must be explained and practiced in a manner children can relate to.

To teach our children to pray, we can gain all the expertise we need from the Bible, the most powerful prayer book we have. In this Holy Book we find Scripture verses encouraging us to pray, teaching us how to pray, providing examples of prayer, and giving us answers to our prayers. Jesus said, "Whatever you ask for in prayer, believe that you have received it, and it will be yours" (Mark 11:24). And on another occasion He said, "Until now you have not asked for anything in my name. Ask and you will receive, and your joy will be complete" (John 16:24).

Pray at a Regular Time Each Day

In our home, dinnertime is the only meal where all the members are present at the table. We take advantage of this gathering of the family and encourage each child to share various joys and concerns with the rest of us. Each evening a different family member closes this sharing with a short thank-you prayer to God. Listening to the prayer needs, we feel a special closeness. For as real-life situations are expressed to other members, it generates an openness and empathy. And pausing to reflect on the greatness of His bounty, we enjoy a prayerful environment where God is alive.

Bedtime prayer is another ritual in our home. At this time, conversation with God is shared between the parent and each child. As the child kneels beside his bed and talks to his Heavenly Father about matters of importance to him, an aura of intimacy develops, linking him not only with his heavenly Parent but his earthly parent as well.

Instead of merely reminding children to pray, we feel it is important to be there with them as they converse with God and establish the discipline of Christian communication.

Speak in a Child's Language

"Our Father, Who art in Heaven, how did you know my name?" Even though the prayer sounds different, the young child merely spoke the words he thought he heard on Sunday morning. Like the missionary in our home who used prayer words that were too remote for our young child, the church can use prayers beyond the comprehension of the children. Old fashioned language only adds to the confusion and mystery of the faith. So we parents take care that our prayers are simple. Try to keep the prayer at a conversational level, expressing needs to God as you talk to Him. A child can interpret your relationship with God as meaningful if the prayer terminology is familiar, ordinary.

Sometimes children may say quite unexpected phrases in their prayers. My daughter prayed at a family reunion after the death of a great-aunt, "Please, God, remind dear Aunt Sarah to feed Ginger" (our dog that had also died recently). I saw beauty in her comprehension of God as Someone she could really talk to and who would listen to her childish, but real, concerns.

Avoid Using Prayer as a Time to Reprimand

Sometimes I have thought about praying at the family meal: "Please, Lord, help my sweet daughter to be more obedient." Don't forget that prayer is communication between a person and God; it should not be used as a gimmick for disciplining others.

Some parents use prayer as a form of punishment. One friend of mine from high school told me that her father would make the most disobedient child in the family pray at dinner each evening. "We grew up hating to pray," she said sadly. "To this day, I still fear closing my eyes and being alone with God."

With prayer in your home, lives can be changed as love is shared between parent and child and as the communion with God deepens. "Prayer is relationship. It is being with God. It is meeting. . . . It is a personal relationship where you and God move from a 'hello' of politeness to an 'embrace' of love. It is communion" (Maxie Dunnam, 21). How can such an act of wholeness and beauty be regarded as punishment? It is our privilege as parents to encourage our children to have the attitude of "I want to pray," instead of "I have to pray."

Talk About Answers to Prayer

"But why did our dog die?" my daughter asked. "I prayed for Ginger to get well. Why did he have to die?"

One of the most difficult tasks as a parent is helping your child cope with situations that do not seem fair. From praying for health and not getting well instantly, to praying for a kitten and not receiving one, children can feel the disappointment of what they believe is unanswered prayer. Parents must continually emphasize that God loves us and understands when we are sad. We need to acknowledge that we do not have all the answers. "I don't know why, but I do know God loves us" may be the best answer one can give.

Communicate with Touch

Touch is an important element in communicating caring to your child during prayer. At the dinner table, we join hands symbolizing the unending circle of God's love in our family. At other times, a hand on the shoulder while we pray communicates our love and concern.

Jesus used touch during His ministry to heal those around Him. We can follow His example with a simple hug or a pat on the back after a bedtime prayer. A bond is formed between parent, child, and God as appropriate physical affection is expressed.

Also thanking God openly for your child helps to affirm his importance as a member of the family and as a child of God. At dinnertime we lift up each member to God, thanking God for his or her uniqueness. The simple, but profound, phrase "Thank You, God, for *(person's name)*" gives each person a feeling of self-worth and spiritual wholeness.

Help Your Child Express Prayers with Personal Meaning

Prayers that arise from your child's heart are important to a young child in feeling that God really understands his special needs. You can help your child experience this as you give situations and ask him to respond in prayer. This teaching experience works well and takes only a few minutes each day. For example:

Situation: Grandmother just fixed your favorite roast beef and you are starving.

Prayer: Thank You, God, for this good food and for my special Grandma.

Situation: Your best friend has the chicken pox and doesn't feel well at all.

Prayer: Please, God, help Cammie to feel better soon so we can go outside and play.

Simple? Yes, but meaningful to a child and to God. Of course, as your child matures, you can explain different ingredients of prayer such as adoration or praise, confessing and asking for forgiveness, thanksgiving, and petitioning for needs of others or self. The prayer formula A.C.T.S. (adoration, confession, thanksgiving, and supplication) is an excellent discipline for anyone as he begins a daily prayer life. As your child begins to understand prayer, encourage him to use the different parts of prayer at bedtime as he praises God for special things, asks for forgiveness, prays for certain needs for others and self, and thanks God for his family.

Be Creative in Prayer

A simple song can be a powerful prayer if the attitude is right. A litany describing feelings on a specific topic can be read by all family members. A Scripture verse can be read as a prayer that pertains to the family situation. By not limiting the types of prayer, we can expand the ways we teach our children to talk with God.

Spend Time Listening to God

Often we become so involved with pouring out troubles and woes that we forget to listen for answers. Remember, God speaks to us in many ways. The Bible tells of God speaking in dreams, visions, and images. Jesus told of God dwelling "within." You need, therefore, to train your children to take time to be still, to hear God speaking during prayer. Encourage family members to keep a paper and pen nearby during their daily prayer and devotion time. As they think of specific needs or of an answer to a concern, ask them to write these down. These thoughts are often a direct answer to prayer about a specific concern.

Expect Miracles to Happen

Prayer is communication with a loving God. Answers to prayer should always be expected. Bring an atmosphere of anticipation to your family as you pray together. Share answers to prayer you have experienced and encourage your children to do the same. A prayer list on a sheet of paper will help members see how God meets requests prayed for. Check the names and concerns from time to time, and discuss the miracle of prayer.

Live a Life of Prayer

Living a life filled with God's love and in communion with God is vital. As the parent, you are commanded to live such a life so your teachings do not become hypocritical.

Encourage your children to pray spontaneously throughout the day as they recognize the love of God in their lives. Verbally acknowledging the beauty of a sunrise, the opening bud on a rosebush, or the first raindrop on a cloudy day can enhance your child's relationship with God. Encourage your young child to see prayer not just as a series of requests, but as a way of life— an agreement, a unity, with our Heavenly Father.

As you talk of God's love, as you try to structure your actions to be like His, your ultimate purpose, which you must role model for your child, is to treat prayer as an ongoing communication. Your child will learn that prayer is not just a two-minute activity, but an all-the-time relationship with a loving Father.

God calls us to pray, for without prayer our life lacks divine direction. When we pray in our homes, together—as a family— we acknowledge that God is a vital part of our life. Teaching our children how to pray through example is one of the most beneficial lessons we can share.

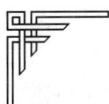 

"Encourage your children to pray spontaneously throughout the day as they recognize the love of God in their lives."

3

The Blessing of the Hummingbird

"[God] will himself restore you and make you strong, firm and steadfast."

—1 Peter 5:10

I couldn't help noticing the disappointment in my husband's eyes as he picked up his briefcase to go to the office that stormy day in August. Although I knew Bob understood why we had to miss our annual retreat to the Carolina mountains, I empathized with him.

Every summer when the hot, humid days in Florida seem as if they will never end, my husband and I have traveled to the cool mountains of North Carolina for our personal retreat. This is the one time each year that we celebrate our life together—no children, no relatives, no friends—just the two of us. Once we arrive at our cabin nestled deep in the lush, green mountainside, our worries seem to diminish. Our perspective on life renews; we become whole again.

Before we even unpack the car, Bob and I go to the old wooden shed and take out all the bird feeding equipment stored from the previous August. We methodically sterilize the empty feeding jars, mix the special sugar water, and fill the containers with this nectar. We hang several of these special hummingbird feeders in the sprawling oak tree next to the cabin's deck and then quietly sit in the wooden rocking chairs as we await our late summer guests. At that moment, we join the ranks of the many avid bird lovers around the world as we marvel at the tiny fluttering creatures in God's kingdom.

As if on a master timer, an hour always passes before one iridescent hummingbird begins to flutter around the feeder to make sure it is safe. Then, just as if the first hummer shouted the news to friends everywhere, more of the tiny jewel-like birds come to satisfy their hunger with the sweet nectar.

For four days in late August each year Bob and I focus on these amazing three-inch creatures. We dress in red shirts, hang strips of red cloth in the tree, and even tie long red ribbons on the porch deck—all to attract these amazing birds. Using high-powered binoculars, we study the reflecting colors on their feathers, observe their flying patterns, and wonder at their voracious appetites.

While waiting for our feathered visitors throughout the days, we talk to each other, share our deepest feelings, and enjoy the tenderness of being alone. Yes, this retreat in August is certainly special.

Until this year. This year because of job conflicts, we couldn't take the time off to go on our annual retreat. For days Bob and I had moped around the house, not daring to voice our disappointment, but feeling each other's emptiness and frustration.

After Bob had left for the office that stormy day, I decided to see if maybe, just maybe, I could attract hummingbirds to our Florida backyard. We had heard from friends who were also hummingbird fans that the tiny bird did not come into our area, and if it did, it was a rare sight for bird watchers indeed.

Hoping for the impossible, I went to the local hardware store and purchased several plastic feeder jars and painted red stripes around the tops and bottoms of them. Methodically, just like on our mountain retreat, I sterilized the jars, mixed the sweet, red sugar water, and filled the feeders to the rim. I then hung them on the limbs of the large tree next to our kitchen patio. Knowing that red seems to attract the hummingbird, I tied several bright-red Christmas aprons to the tree and even hung a large red overnight bag near the feeder.

Someone looking into our backyard could have thought I had lost my mind; nevertheless, attracting the birds would be worth it. *Maybe we can create our mountain retreat right in our back-*

yard, I thought. Maybe the hummingbirds would be attracted to our home.

When Bob walked in the door that evening, he still seemed out-of-sorts, moody—until he noticed the backyard. "What in the world have you done?" he asked in amazement as he stared at the feeders of red nectar and the bright red fabrics waving in the breeze. "You know the birds rarely come to this part of the state."

"Well, it's worth a try," I said hopefully. "Besides, what do we have to lose?"

We both must have been hopeful, for that evening we sat expectantly at the kitchen patio while eating dinner. We could not take our eyes off the decorated tree. We had our dessert at the kitchen patio and even chose to watch the sunset instead of television that evening. We talked quietly and found ourselves laughing and unwinding, as if we were at our mountain retreat. In spite of our hopes, no hummingbirds appeared.

The next morning was the same. Nothing ate the nectar; nothing flew in sight. As Bob left for work looking a bit despondent, he just had to mention it: "You know that today is when we were supposed to leave for the mountains."

That did it. I just had to lure a hummingbird to our home. I went to the local nursery and purchased some bright cardinal flowers and planted them around the kitchen patio. My obsession with attracting the tiny bird was becoming noticeable to neighbors, who began peering over our wooden fence that afternoon.

"Excuse me, Mrs. Bruce. Are you trying to decorate for Christmas in August?" one neighbor asked slyly.

Another neighbor commented on how my red "flags" didn't go with the yellow brick on my home, and my daughter's friend wanted to know if we were having a belated Fourth of July party. I didn't let the humorous comments hinder my efforts. I was determined to attract a tiny hummer.

Late that afternoon, just about the same time we had been scheduled to arrive at our mountain retreat, I was washing dishes in the kitchen. I glanced outside at the shady tree, longing for a tiny bird to fly toward my feeder, when I thought I saw something shiny on the cardinal plant. Was it a shiny butterfly fluttering around? I leaned closer to the window to get a better look. It wasn't a butterfly; it was a hummingbird! We had attracted to our backyard the most gorgeous ruby-throated hummer I had ever seen .

I quietly perched myself at the kitchen table to watch the bird flutter and feed, only to see it fly away immediately. *I know it will come back,* I thought; *it just has to.*

Bob arrived home about an hour later. I couldn't wait to tell him about the visit of the hummer. "It really did fly around the feeder," I said excitedly. "Maybe it didn't feed, but it was here."

I knew he was a bit skeptical, but we took our places at the "lookout" table and stared at the tree. About an hour had passed when we finally saw action in the air. Not one, not two, but five hummingbirds were flying around the red fabrics and the tempting feeders. They were flying up, down, sideways, and even upside down as they tried to suck the sweet nectar from the jars.

As we held hands and watched the aerial acrobatics, Bob smiled with satisfaction while I laughed with a feeling of fulfillment. The hummingbirds had really come to our home—and on the very day we would have observed them in the mountains. We felt content; our August retreat was complete.

For the past five years, Bob and I had sought this mystical bird sanctuary far away from our daily lives. We had planned, prepared, and driven miles to capture a brief four days of the hummingbird's marvelous habits. Then after leaving our mountain retreat, we would wait all year in anticipation of experiencing this moment again. Only now did we realize the bird was in our backyard all the time.

The blessing of the tiny hummingbird taught me an unforgettable lesson about God. Don't we all yearn for that mountaintop experience, that exhilarating spiritual high, that perfect retreat, with Him? We may make plans and preparations to meet with God and search the world over to find Him when all we need to do is realize He is with us all the time.

4
Time Out to Be with God

"Jesus . . . went off to a solitary place, where he prayed."
—Mark 1:36

If your family is like ours, you are probably going too fast in too many directions. It seems that the older our children get, the less time we spend together celebrating our Christian faith and family bond. In fact, a typical family evening that used to involve talking to each other, sharing our thoughts about the events of our day, is more often like this:

"Rob, please slow down. You are going to choke on your spaghetti," my husband would say patiently.

"Can't, Dad. Gotta hurry and go. Coach wants to take us to batting practice till nine tonight," Rob would say between giant bites of food. "Can I just take a few pieces of bread and go now?"

"And I'm not really hungry," my middle daughter would chime in. "We made ice cream sundaes at Kristin's this afternoon. Besides, I need to go work on my science project at Julie's house at seven o'clock. It's due tomorrow."

And the youngest seemed to be caught up in the hurried moment. "Mom, do I have to eat with you and Daddy? This is so boring! Can I take my plate into the den and watch cartoons?"

I realize that breaking ties is inevitable the older our children get and the more they become oriented to their peers. And I also understand that school activities, sports, projects, and clubs have their place in a child's development. But I still feel that as

Christian parents we have a continuing challenge and responsibility to offer spiritual discipline and religious training to our young.

In Deuteronomy 6:4–7, we read, "And you shall teach this to your children . . ." But as I saw my three children rushing to various activities, I realized that to abide by this Scripture passage, to encourage spiritual maturity, we had to pull together even more as a family. Since time was becoming a factor with each family member, my husband and I planned a Time-Out as a daily religious training and worship experience for our family.

Time-Out is used in most sports events. In boxing, when the punches get too violent, or one person needs relief, the referee calls a time-out. In football, if there is a scuffle on the field or a player is injured, a time-out is called.

The Bible affirms a slowing down, a getting away, by mentioning various times that our Lord retreated to be alone with himself and His Heavenly Father.

For a busy family with older children, a Time-Out each day to focus on sharing God's love and concern is wonderful for getting your children's prayer and spiritual life on the right track of Christian discipline. This family time can be before breakfast or after dinner or whatever time is best suited for your children's needs. Yet this time should be practiced daily.

Because worship is a Christian celebration, as well as being reverent, this Time-Out with God should be appealing to your children, having a positive tone. In beginning Time-Outs, we sang rounds of the children's favorite songs, played Bible relays, and shared light moments in their daily lives. This attitude of enjoyment is vital as the children are developing what faith means to them.

Memorization of Scripture verses was another important tool. Once the children began to memorize several key Scripture verses, our family began to play Bible relay games. As computer buffs, we found several exciting computer games that used questions on the Scriptures and the life of Jesus. The children started becoming more interested in their faith-history as they challenged themselves and each other. After several weeks, our challenge to spend a Time-Out with God became longer as the children dug deeper into the Scriptures with the computer game. (Check with computer stores in your area for games that fit your particular computer.)

At the same time, during our Time-Out, one of the things we did was teach the Bible. We realized that merely saying the Scriptures as a family unit was not adequate for its life-message to be understood. We related the passages we read to situations in each child's life and asked the children to try to do the same. For example, if we talked about giving during our family together time, we discussed feelings the children had about giving their time to others, giving their money to the church, and sharing with each other. We found that by applying the Scriptures to their individual situations, our children began to see how the Bible was a personal guide for successful living, not just a black book Mom and Dad thought was important.

Drama was a fun learning experience in our family Time-Out. We involved the children by making up a story and asking them to act out the situation. We challenged them to remember Scripture passages that would assist them. As they acted out the mini-skit, they were able to see how the other person felt. These feelings were remembered for later days when similar situations actually happened to them. Noticeable changes in their behavior occurred: The children began to respond with empathy and compassion.

Prayer was vital as we thanked God for bringing us together. We explained prayer as conversation with God and encouraged the children to speak in their own words and language. Trying to memorize prayers was not for us; we wanted the children to know God on a personal basis. We kept a prayer list within our immediate family, lifting up personal needs, friends who were ill, and other concerns. We also checked the list periodically to see how the prayers were answered. Yes, they were answered! If a prayer wasn't answered the way our children thought it should have been, that became an opportunity to discuss their feelings openly. We tried to explain that God's plan was not always our plan and encouraged spiritual growth even in times of disappointment.

Sharing our faith as adults was especially meaningful with our children during Time-Out. My husband and I would tell of times when God became real to us as children (or teenagers or young adults). We shared our feelings of loneliness without God and how His presence enabled us to feel complete in our Christian journey. We let our children know that God was continuing to work in our adult lives, and we shared blessings that we experienced each day.

When ups and downs occurred in our lives, our Time-Out became instrumental in explaining them. For example, when my husband was transferred to another city to continue his ministry, Time-Out, where the children were open with their feelings, offered the perfect opportunity to tell of the move. We prayed for guidance and help so the children would understand the calling and strength of God in our lives.

Most importantly, in our Time-Out we were able to use the quiet moments of solitude for reflecting on self. One evening we sat as a family on the back porch and just watched the colorful Florida sunset. Without saying any Scripture passages or prayers or sharing any feelings, we all experienced God's power through the beauty of His world.

After establishing our special time amid our busy schedule, we began to encourage our children to be alone with their thoughts throughout the day. We suggested that they read Scripture passages, keep a personal prayer list for friends, and write down thoughts or questions they may want answers to later.

Our Time-Out has become a family tradition. The Scripture passages we shared have been carried over into our children's lives as they interact with peers. Caring, forgiving, and turning the other cheek have become character traits of our children.

Recently I shared with my neighbor about our family's worship time amid our hectic schedule. "We started with just a few minutes each day being together as a family with God," I explained to her.

Her personal religious beliefs baffled me.

"Not our family! I am going to let my children make their own religious decisions," she said flatly. "When they are grown, they can decide about worship, reading the Bible, going to church, and believing in God."

Would we allow our children to grow up without learning to read or going to school? What parent would let his children become malnourished by not providing a proper well-balanced diet? If we provide for their physical needs, how can we let them starve for spiritual training and nourishment within the family?

Just as good nutrition is necessary for the body and academic training is vital for a vocation, spiritual training in the home is necessary to your child if he is to grow up making responsible, ethical decisions. The responsibility of this training is not totally in the hands of the Sunday school teacher or pastor. Certainly it is not to be left to whoever would influence our children in the world at large! It is in our hands, the parents, through daily nurture and a life-style that exhibits God's love and care.

The psalmist writes, "Be still and know that I am God" (Psalm 46:10). To truly realize this, to find the unending source of strength, renewal, and encouragement we need to live, we must set the example of our Lord by helping our children experience solitude and worship in the home. Then as our children begin to listen to God through prayer, through study, and through others, they can discover their inner spiritual resources and use them to tell others about God's grace.

Time-Out worked for our family in teaching our children how to have a daily quiet time. The results will be eternal!

5

For Aunt Bub

"With long life will I satisfy him."

—Psalm 91:16

When I was a young girl, I hated vegetables. I remember balking at the crisp, green cabbage on my plate and hearing my mother say, "If you won't eat them to stay healthy, then eat them for Aunt Bub." So I ate them, and I still do.

"Vegetables are the secret to a long, healthy life," my Aunt Bub would say to me as I spent the long summer days on her Florida farm. She spoke from experience, for she had lived a long, healthy life. Even though she was only fifty when I was ten, Aunt Bub was the oldest person in the world, or at least the oldest person I had ever known, and the wisest too.

When I was lucky enough to spend the night with her, I would secretly set my alarm for seven to try to wake up before this slight bundle of energy. But when my alarm would go off, I always awoke to the aroma of hot coffee, and pancakes on the griddle.

Aunt Bub would be ready for the day wearing a faded cotton house dress and a bright red apron. The table would be ready for a feast with large, whole strawberries, fresh squeezed orange juice, and her prized tomatoes sliced delectably thin.

"You've gotta get up with the chickens on a farm," she would tell me matter-of-factly as I lazily wiped the sleep from my eyes. "The day is half over, and you've already missed the best part. Youngun', you're just too 'city-fied.'"

At that point, she would serve my breakfast and quickly return to her morning duties in the large vegetable garden.

Ah, her prized vegetable garden—butter beans, tomatoes, collards, and corn, cabbages, carrots, peppers, and potatoes. If it could be grown in the fine Florida sand, Aunt Bub planted it, grew it, and grew it well. Throughout the morning hours, I would play on the old tire swing hanging from the ageless oak tree and watch this amazing woman work. She did the work of an army of strong men as she shucked corn, shelled peas, snapped beans, and picked tiny green bugs off large leafs of greens. She hauled baskets of green and yellow peppers to her house for freezing and returned with empty baskets for the new crop of Florida cabbages. Throughout the morning, she sheared, sorted, weeded, and watered. She dug, divided, pared, and pruned. Aunt Bub treated her vegetables with the delicate touch of a master gardener.

"Take these cukes over to the creek behind the barn and stick them in the water between the rocks so they can cool off," she would say. "We'll stop our work in a bit and have a snack."

Normally I avoided these long, smooth, green vegetables, but these were Aunt Bub's cucumbers straight from her magical garden; they were different.

After about an hour, she would walk over to the spring-fed creek and sit on the moss-covered rocks under the tall pines. Taking her thick straw sun hat, Aunt Bub would dip it into the water, using it like a basin. Icy water splashed over her dirt and sweat-covered face, renewing the impish twinkle in her dark brown eyes. She then pulled a tiny pocket knife out of her apron and with seeming magic, she sliced the cooled cucumbers into perfect fourths.

"Now listen to me," she would say, smiling as she devoured her natural snack. "If you eat this, you'll always stay healthy when you grow old like me."

Somehow, after I ate my share, I did feel a bit more energized and alive.

Afternoons were spent taking naps as the Florida sun forced itself on the tiny farm. The rhythmic squeak of the wooden porch swing combined with the soft hum of the large electric fan to lull both of us to sleep until loud thunder from a nearby storm would call us back to life.

The evening hours were spent around the antique pine table as friends and relatives stopped by to meet "Bub's niece."

The table spread would put a "city" Thanksgiving dinner to shame. Garden fresh green beans, collard greens, buttered lima beans, corn on the cob, and corn off the cob. Succulent steamed okra with tomatoes, black-eyed peas served with rice, and the largest cantaloupes I had ever seen. The meats were simple: baked chicken, savory meat loaf, and fresh fish caught in a neighbor's pond. And the breads were hot from the oven: buttermilk biscuits, and of course, corn bread.

Believe me when I say that vegetables had never tasted like this before. I remember putting just one of each kind on my plate just to be polite, but before I knew it I was having seconds and thirds of these amazing foods.

After the hungry bunch ate this feast, they moved to the open porch and planted their stuffed, bloated bodies in the creaking rocking chairs. The conversation went something like this:

"Did you hear about Erma Johnson's Cousin Myrtle?" said one great-uncle, tempting the group as he blew smoke from his pipe into the steamy evening air.

"Naw," another uncle replied as he slapped a pesky mosquito. "What's that girl gone and done now?"

And the story of neighbor Erma Johnson's Cousin Myrtle leaving her small hometown to take a job in New York as an attorney was told and retold. Heads were shaking and sighs of reproach could be heard.

"It's not good, she'll see," Aunt Bub would mutter under her breath. "I knew her mama back when, and she always wanted to go to the big city too."

Then that special mischievous twinkle in her dark brown eyes appeared again, and she announced with pride that it was time for dessert—Bub's homemade ice cream.

"Fresh peach ice cream, and homemade!" The men folk beamed as they savored the creamy orange and white confection in their mouths. "Nobody makes fresh peach ice cream like Bub."

Aunt Bub would wink at me; only she and I shared her secret recipe. Early that morning, she had taken out the gallon of Bryan's Dairy ice milk she bought at the local grocery store the day before. She softened the ice milk and mixed fresh, sliced peaches in it. Aunt Bub then carefully packed the store-bought concoction in the metal container from her old ice cream maker hiding it deep in the freezer.

"We'll now call it homemade," she had said laughingly to me hours ago. "They don't need that rich homemade ice cream with all those fats. Youngun', no one will ever know."

Instead of spending her morning sweating and churning ice cream for the evening's company, Aunt Bub spent it doing what she liked best, working with God's bountiful food in her prized vegetable garden.

Today I prod my three children with the same words of wisdom, "Eat your vegetables! If you won't do it to stay healthy, then do it for Aunt Bub." And believe it or not, they eat them.

There must be something to it. Long before health reports came out claiming the wondrous disease-fighting benefits of vegetables, we had been encouraged our entire lives to eat our vegetables "to stay healthy and because Aunt Bub eats them."

"Vegetables are the secret to a long, healthy life," Aunt Bub wisely told me while eating cucumbers at her creek over thirty years ago. And this year sprightly Aunt Bub still works hard in her prized vegetable garden on that Central Florida farm as she celebrates eighty years of amazingly healthy living.

That says something, doesn't it? But more than that, I hope that your child has an "Aunt Bub," an older person whom they can visit, someone who will help you make memories for your child that will count.

6

Be a Storyteller

"They received the message with great eagerness and examined the Scriptures every day."

—Acts 17:11

"But Mommy, I don't understand it." My young daughter honestly didn't understand the meaning of the Bible verse I had read to her. Figurative phrases like "light of the world" and "salt of the earth" just didn't make sense to an eight-year-old. But these phrases were important both to her and to me.

Have you ever read a Scripture passage to your children at bedtime only to realize you needed more practical examples to explain the biblical message to them? Or when interpreting the Scriptures to your child, perhaps you have drawn a blank in making the Scripture passages relevant.

Teaching our children the stories in the Bible or referring to scriptural examples is one of the oldest ways of communicating our Christian faith. Our Lord told parables to crowds of people as He shared about God's love. These parables, or stories with a message, helped to explain the Bible in terms the people could understand. The Indians also used storytelling to teach their people. Many years ago entire tribes would sit around the campfire at night and listen to captivating stories that taught them how to live and love.

In our families we learn of our heritage and traditions from listening to personal stories handed down through the generations. In fact, the favorite phrase at bedtime in most homes is often, "Please! Just one more story."

Using real-life stories and personal experiences can enhance your biblical teaching in the family. These examples can often make Scripture passages clearer, more relevant to today's life, and convincing to the point of a personal response from your children.

We should recognize that people are interested in people. When you use a story about a real life situation involving real people, you can perk up a child's interest. Your children can relate to a character in the story or to a predicament being faced. Their ownership of the character and the predicament occurs as your children hear a vivid background description and get involved in the developing plot.

Biblical terms that may be too abstract for the young child can be interpreted through telling a personal story. Yet telling stories and sharing personal experiences at home is not as easy as it may seem. Perhaps the following suggestions could help you bring the Bible to life as you enhance your child's understanding of Scripture passages and relate the message of the Gospels with effective examples.

Make It True

Stories that aren't true sound invented. Somehow, human nature is extremely fine-tuned and can tell fact from fable. You may ask, How can I find an example to explain Scripture passages if I don't make it up? Let's look at several key ways.

Get Personal

The most convincing examples are those you have experienced. Begin by keeping a personal journal or an "encounter" book. Each day jot down experiences or insights that you have where God has been made known to you. Write down your questions, doubts, and fears, as well as your answers to prayer and spiritual awakenings. Then as you read the Bible to your children in the evening, reflect on this journal and find situations that might relate to the emphasis of the Scripture passage.

You don't have to be the hero or heroine of the story each week! Perhaps God became real to you through your mistake or failure. Don't tell the story with the intention of glorifying yourself. Rather, look for anecdotes that help to glorify God.

Collect Examples

Listen to people talk around you—at home, church, work, or play. Write in your journal interesting experiences you may hear about where God became real in the lives of others. Avoid using anecdotes or stories that would embarrass anyone. Changing the names of real people is appropriate. As you lead into the story you might say, "Something like this happened to a friend." This would help to avoid using names.

Another excellent resource for finding suitable examples and stories to tell your children is in Christian magazines, books, and the local newspaper. Clip out relevant information and articles or jot down the particulars, and keep these in your journal.

Make It Specific

An example that is spoken in generalities is far less believable than one spoken in specific terms. For example, if you say, "Several people have used prayer in their lives with miraculous results," you have hardly convinced your children. If you say, "Listen to the miraculous answers this man tells about in this magazine article about his struggle with prayer," even the most rebellious teenager or distracted child will tune in and become more convinced of the message you are trying to teach. Your believability increases as you describe particular incidents in detail.

Make Your Story Active

You do not need to memorize the story or example word for word; in fact, you will be more effective if you study and understand the message of the account. A clear understanding of the characters—their names, their personalities, their relationships with each other—is important. A grasp of the sequence of action you're going to tell about, and its background, is also important to your retelling.

If you become uncertain of details in relating an anecdote or story to your children, read directly from the article, book, or your journal, where the story is recorded.

It has been said that practice makes perfect. In telling a story to help your children understand biblical truths, practice may help you feel at ease in sharing the example. As you repeat the words over and over, you become secure with the material. This adds to your believability. Always relate how the Scripture passage was important for the people or situation involved in the story.

Make It Relate to the Scripture Verses You Read

Ask yourself, How does this story relate to the verses I am reading to my children? You must consciously sort through your life, your journal, and your collection of examples and find the specific anecdotes that can enhance the verses you read and your personal goals for this Bible passage.

Make the Story an Experience

Children become even more familiar with the story you are trying to teach if you allow them to experience it in a variety of ways.

The story may be written on cards and used as a role-play or mini drama for the children to act out. As they take on the various roles of the characters, they can interpret the story as one with meaning in their own life. You may prepare questions to ask your children regarding the meaning of the role-play after they are through. Talk with your children about the story you read or that they act out so the meaning is clear.

You or your children may wear costumes to give more emphasis to the story being told. Props can be added to the costumed characters to give even more credence to the story. For example, if the story is about a woman who encountered God while traveling alone one night on a trip, you might use a prop such as an overnight case to add interest to the story. This will allow your children to feel more of what the character in the story was feeling.

If you find you can't tell stories to your children without losing your train of thought, you can always tape-record the various stories and play the tape to the children. You may have various friends or family members record the voices on the tapes, use background music for added emphasis, and fill in when necessary with the narration of the story, giving location, time, place, and other important specifics. The added benefit of taped stories is that children can listen to them when you are away.

Storytelling is an important method for sharing God's Word in the family. Using examples and stories to add a personal touch to your children's devotional time is a sure way to gain the attention of even the youngest child. By using a little preparation, practice, and prayer, you can become an effective storyteller. Then, by following the suggestions mentioned, you can help bring the Bible to life in your home, resulting in new understanding, added enthusiasm for God's Word, and changed lives.

7

Adventures in Family Devotions

"Speak to one another with psalms, and hymns and spiritual songs. Sing and make music in your heart to the Lord."
—Ephesians 5:19

Worshiping as a family while seated on a comfortable pew in church is standard for most Christians. The quietness of the stained-glass sanctuary, the soothing chords from the organ, and the choir's majestic anthem all add to the worship environment. Yet when we try to have meaningful worship with our family in the home, we often have difficulty capturing the same atmosphere. Our thoughts are interrupted by phones ringing, cars honking, the dog scratching on the back door, and children moving about.

Worship is communion with God. It is also our response to God's love. This response is a vital part of the Christian family's life-style. As we make time to worship Christ as our Savior, we affirm our love for Him. Our children begin to develop faith as they listen to us Christian parents share what God means in our lives. Our family ties strengthen as we tune into the daily joys and concerns of each member.

How can you begin to have devotional times in the home as a family? There are numerous ideas in books and magazines about how to have family devotions; yet how do you keep the attention and dedication of the different ages involved?

How can we guide our family in meaningful devotion time?

1. Begin one step at a time. Often, well-meaning Christians decide to begin family devotions and have them each night of the week. This is excellent if the family willingly commits the time and energy to follow through; however, one night a week may be more realistic and effective for beginning the devotional habit. By carefully coordinating it with busy schedules, this one night could be so creatively planned that family members begin to look forward to the next devotion night. It is better to begin with a definite commitment of one night a week than to lose interest by trying too much too soon.

2. Plan the devotion thoroughly. Have a purpose or theme in mind before the family sits down together. This could be a study of God's love, grace, or forgiveness, or the life of Jesus. Study the theme you have chosen, focusing on the Scripture passages each day before the family devotion. You may choose to post the theme and the Scripture passages on the refrigerator so other members of the family can relate their lives to them. Be prepared to share a personal incident that makes the passage meaningful.

3. Come with expectation! You can bring expectation and excitement to your family devotion as you look for small, daily accomplishments of family members and affirm them. I remember when young Ashley brought me a rose on Monday after preschool, when Britt prayed aloud for the first time, when Rob was able to look up a Scripture verse on his own. Being hopeful and sharing the unexpected pleasures in life help the family devotion come alive.

4. Set a specific time and stick to it. It is easy to say, "We're all too tired tonight." Yet a definite day and time is a must for establishing the devotional habit in the family. If you encourage promptness, the family will begin to make it a point to remember the date and time and include it in their regular routine. On the other hand, changing the devotion to different times each week weakens commitment to it.

5. Welcome discussion during the family devotion. This is a time when each member can openly question the topic or add personal insights to the Scripture passage. In our home, the older children enjoy Scripture study, using their own Bibles, but not our younger daughter, who is quickly bored. Realizing this, we gear each Scripture passage or topic to her age-level and

share simple truths she can relate to, such as "We show our love for God when we share." Making the Scripture come to life calls for involvement from each member.

6. Try to provide an environment in the home where grace can be experienced. This involves smooth transition between family discussion, the sharing of joys and concerns, and praying for others. An environment of grace requires that family members be caring people and help each other feel that love and concern.

7. Use creative methods in your family devotional. Use props, puppets, Bible quizzes, relays, songs, and movement. Family devotions do not have to be all lecture by one person. The more involved each member is, the more likely the message will be ingrained in his or her life.

8. Don't openly criticize any family member during the devotion. Accentuate the positive and handle any discipline problems quietly. If one child insists on demonstrating unacceptable behavior, ask him to leave the room; discuss the problem with him at a later time. You represent God to your family as you lead them in worship. Your loving-kindness must be displayed as you train them.

9. Don't come to the devotion time with a negative attitude. Begin each session with prayer and oneness with God. Try to leave all problems and worries out of the experience.

10. Don't be afraid to let God use you during the devotion. Be open to the power of the Holy Spirit as you lead. If you feel an urge to pray during the study, then pray! If you feel led to share or to sing, then do so joyously! Avoid becoming so structured with your devotional plan that you ignore those special moments when God intervenes.

11. Don't forget to allow times for sharing needs within the family—for prayer requests. Keeping a family prayer list and posting it someplace in the home enables the members to take this communication seriously. As answers to prayer occur, the family members can see God at work in their lives.

12. Don't let the devotion time become boring. Be prepared with more activities, questions, and Scripture studies than the time will allow. This devotion time in the family is so vital for spiritual growth that you need to fill it to the brim!

13. Don't appear too pious or self-righteous. It is important

that you be approachable during the family devotion. If your faith seems real to your children, they will model it in their lives.

After you get into the habit of once-a-week family devotions, then consider twice a week. Set spiritual goals for your family for a three-month period, a six-month period, and a twelve-month period. Measure the interest, enthusiasm, and participation of each devotional time. Make necessary changes as the stages in your family's life changes.

Devotions can be one of the most exciting adventures a Christian family can enjoy. This adventure begins with loving parents who care enough to plan the sessions and provide an environment in the home where God's grace can be shared.

8

"Can't I Skip Church?"

"Let us not give up meeting together . . . but let us encourage one another."

—Hebrews 10:25

I have a difficult time with many of my friends who allow their children to make choices regarding their spiritual life. For example, my friend Wanda is afraid to "make" her thirteen-year-old son go to church against his will.

"There are so many things in life that John 'must' do that I just feel like going to church shouldn't be forced upon him," Wanda said sincerely. "After all, if I make him go when he doesn't want to, he may grow up to resent this and never go to church as an adult."

Other friends with older children and teens agree with her. "I was made to go to church with my family every Sunday morning, Sunday evening, and Wednesday night," another friend, Bob, said after a weekend fishing trip with the guys. "Now I resent church and would rather spend my time fishing on Sunday morning."

This attitude bothers me. I was also brought up in a Christian home with both parents active in our local church. On Sunday morning my parents "made" us go when it was much more appealing to lay sleepily in bed. Did we smile and like it? No. I remember some Sunday mornings as a rebellious fifteen-year-old when I resented this authority in my life. But looking back, I now know my parents' discipline and faith in God ultimately became my discipline and personal faith.

When we moved two years ago to a new city where my husband was appointed senior pastor of a large church, we were confronted with the question of do we make them go to church? As the parents of two teenagers and one close behind, periodically we had faced this battle of "Can't I skip church, just today?" While driving to our new appointment, we discussed openly the family rules on spiritual discipline.

"Now I want to remind you, there will be no battles on Sunday morning," my husband said firmly. "You guys will all get up, get dressed, and get to Sunday school on time."

"Well, Dad, I just want to warn you," our teenage son, Rob, said assertively, "you will not make me go to youth group or to that youth choir they have. I'll go to church 'cause I know that is the rule, but this time I will make my own choice about anything else I belong to, okay?"

"Yeah, me too," his younger sister Brittnye chimed in. "You can't make us do what we don't want to do. It's our life."

Looking back at my two teens, I clearly saw determination in their dark eyes. But our answer was the same as it had been throughout their lives: "You will go to church. And you will find other groups to become members of."

To some people, the thought of forcing a child to take this spiritual journey and accept this kind of discipline seems harsh. It is our belief that just as you make children go to school during the week to learn the three Rs, you make them go to church on Sunday to learn about God. Since we didn't give them a choice about school, why should we give them a choice about church?

The idea of going to church as a spiritual discipline for children and teenagers has good reasons. Recent studies show that children who stay with the local church through the ninth grade may break away during college or early career, but most will come back when their own children are young. As we look around in our congregation, we can see the young adults with babies and toddlers coming back into the church as they begin to take seriously the responsibility of raising a family. Most of these young adults were active in churches when they were children. Some admittedly did stray away during college and career, but are now coming back and actively joining committees, classes, and study groups.

There are more reasons for wanting our children to be active in a local church. We have found that commitment to a Sunday school class or a youth program—a specific body of believers—is also important to complete and complement their development as Christian young people. Class membership means being accountable to serve on committees, to find their talents and use them in class, and to attend faithfully.

This commitment to a youth class has enhanced their relationship with other young Christians and with our family members. As our children learned to listen to the ideas of others and compromise in making decisions, they learned to accept each other.

Studying the Scriptures at worship, in Sunday school, and during their youth program gives our children insight into life. Through the Bible, they are able to understand each other and find guidance for living a more Christlike life. The beauty of searching God's Word within the fellowship of the church is that other caring adults, not just their parents, are able to share how He has revealed himself in their lives. They can also learn from the experiences of young Christians around them.

Our children have found a supportive community in their class. Their friends and teachers have shown them love and compassion when their sister faced surgery, support when a tragic death struck a favorite uncle, and joy as they encountered success in their school work.

Community is further experienced by our children in the small-group Bible study their youth minister teaches. The delightful part of the growing friendships made during this time is that age and sex are not barriers. In their study group they experienced caring friendships with girls and boys of all ages.

Going to church has added strength to our children, especially as they moved into a new community. Where members of the congregation work to know each other, our children seem to always experience care and concern, two qualities vital to their Christian maturity.

Through their youth Sunday school class, they have been challenged to change for Christ. Decisions to be more Christlike have been nurtured as they have met for fellowship and study.

Well, we moved into our new parsonage. Our three stubborn children went to church the first Sunday. They grudgingly tried the new youth group and choir. The following week, they asked us to take them to the youth group. They even tried out for the small-group ensemble, which rehearsed late on Sunday evenings. The next week, they asked to go a bit earlier to youth group to play Frisbee golf with some friends and stayed after ensemble practice to work on a new bell-choir. Two months later, all three children were elected by their peers to serve on the Youth Council.

We've been in our new situation for several years now. The battle is over for a while as our children are actively involved in our new congregation. They might choose to make different decisions when they go away to college, but we know that as their parents we are giving them the greatest gift of all—spiritual discipline.

Do you make your child go to church or do you give him a choice each week? The decision is yours, but in our home our children's spiritual discipline and Christian pilgrimage is a priority. What is our Sunday morning reply? "Yes, you will go to church!"

9

When Disappointment Rolls In

"In this world you will have trouble. But take heart! I have overcome the world."

—John 16:33

Has anyone in your family faced disappointment or failure recently? Perhaps the letdown came when a special vacation had to be postponed for lack of money or when a family member failed to keep his promise. Maybe a family member lost his job during the recession and could not maintain the life-style the members were used to. Whatever the case, everyone, even Christian families, face disappointment or failure at some time.

Often family disappointments result when the members expect too much of an event. When these high expectations are not met, disappointment occurs.

When our close friends John and Anita prepared their two children for a recent move to a nearby coastal city, they tried to get the children excited by telling them their new home might have a swimming pool.

"We wanted to promise them almost anything to help them look forward to moving," John said later. "After pricing the homes with pools, we found we could not afford this added luxury and had to buy a house without one. We felt terrible, but seeing the kids' disappointment was almost more than we could stand."

Disappointment or feelings of frustration can occur in the

most loving families when one member forgets to fulfill an expected responsibility, such as a household chore. Seventeen-year-old Jason had promised his parents that he would take care of the yard during the summer months. When summer came, Jason chose to work long hours at a nearby restaurant.

"We depended on Jason to help us with the yard work, but after three weeks it became apparent that his new job and social life were more important than our family," his father said sadly. "We finally had to hire a lawn service to take over Jason's responsibility."

These feelings of frustration and despair also occur in families when goals are set too high for the members and are not met. Our family experienced this letdown recently when we agreed to save money to purchase a video recorder this year and failed to meet our goal.

Self-pity often enters into situations such as these where disappointments are harbored by family members and are not dealt with in the right way. After Sara took her new job with the city newspaper, she became a different person at home.

"I'd always wanted to be a reporter," she said. "I was hired to do secretarial work. At the interview the editor promised I could write articles from time to time. After being on the job for two months, he finally admitted that my writing was not up to par for their publication. I was devastated, but worse than that, my disappointment and negative attitude was taken out on members of my family."

Family members who face disappointment often begin to feel as if the world is against them. They sometimes become oversensitive as they are engulfed in this defeated attitude. Apathy may spread from one member to another, and the general attitude of all members can become negative. More disappointments will usually follow as members make halfhearted attempts at their goals in life.

You can help your family members grow through times of disappointments. Faith in a living God calls for hope during times of trial. You can interpret this faith by suggesting ways of dealing positively with various disappointments.

Scripture passages can assist you in this guidance. Paul's letter to the Romans emphasizes the importance of hope rising above failure. In Romans 12:1–2, Paul urges us to seek God's will, accepting that which is just and right. Again in Romans Paul offers advice in dealing with disappointment, saying, "Never pay back evil for evil." Throughout the Old and New Testaments are accounts of people who struggled with life's trials and tribulations. The stories demonstrate how God gave strength and hope to those who asked.

Dealing with disappointment in this positive manner is not easy. With guidance from God's Word and open communication, however, you can help those you love to learn from these events lessons that relate to their personal lives.

Ways To Deal With Family Disappointments

Maybe the following questions can offer some encouragement during times of defeat.

- Can family members talk openly about disappointments?

Bottled-up negative feelings only continue to grow. But talking about disappointments in the Christian home helps to ease the tension and anxiety they created. As family members share their feelings of resentment and anger, the disappointment seems to lessen, and it soon becomes a part of the past.

As you hold periodic family discussions, ask, "What were the expectations you had for the event? What was the resulting situation? What could have made it different? Can you still recover from this thwarted expectation and seek a new interest or goal?"

Empathy and caring can take place as these concerns and feelings are communicated. Personal goals can be restated and family members can begin anew.

- How can we find God amid disappointment?

As Christians, we know that through prayer, Bible study, and listening to God through others, we can find God's plan for us.

Did the disappointment jeopardize a planned goal? When our family failed to save enough money for the video recorder to take on vacation, we all were disappointed. We had looked forward to capturing the white-water rafting trip on film and enjoying this in later years. To deal with disappointment in a way that encourages growth, we had to seek other options. We settled on purchasing a good camera for a lot less money, and took pictures that we displayed in a vacation album. Often when one plan is thwarted (bringing feelings of frustration), other options are possible or new opportunities present themselves. In our case, we searched for more workable options and were satisfied with the result.

- Can we use the strength the Lord gives to move on in our lives?

Major disappointments bring anguish in life, causing a person to feel his world has fallen in. Yet God does give strength to begin anew. Fellowship and communication within the family are vital; strength can come from within this tight-knit unit.

As you help your family members deal with disappointments, avoid getting on their same level. When our daughter came home from school and tearfully announced that she didn't make the solo in the Christmas pageant, my first reaction was to call the music director and find out why. After some thought, I realized this disappointment was just one of many she would have in life. She would have to learn to deal with it gracefully and positively. Instead of calling the school, we went into the kitchen and shared a snack as I laughingly told her about my own disappointments in middle school.

One friend has a sign in her kitchen that says, "When life gives you lemons, make lemonade." She said, "I always try to help the kids make something good out of the disappointments in their life. If they get their minds off themselves and begin to reach out to help someone else, they will find fulfillment."

- Can we forgive those who disappoint us?

The essence of the gospel message is loving and forgiving. Because we do not forgive, we often collect feelings of anguish after disappointing situations.

By placing our faith in God, building our lives on His Word through continual prayer, fellowship, and service, we can experience the strength to forgive those who hurt or disappoint us. Accepting others where they are instead of molding them into persons we want them to be helps to eliminate frustration and disappointment. This selfless love becomes a reality as we allow it to generate acceptance, forgiveness, and spiritual growth, and as we place our complete faith in God instead of humankind.

My neighbor Sara was finally able to accept her job and forgive her boss for misleading her at the newspaper. "I kept thinking, 'Let the one who is without sin' criticize. I knew I had many shortcomings and had probably treated others in a similar way in the past. I became willing to forgive my boss and move on with my life, doing my best on the job. My attitude has changed, and even my writing has improved."

So how do you deal with disappointment when it faces a family member? Do you and the rest of the family blame it on others? Or do you accept disappointment as a part of life and move on toward more positive goals? Do you see disappointment as a closed door, or do you seek the challenge that exists as new doors wait to be opened?

The Scriptures never promised that our lives would be without disappointment. But God's Word does offer us acceptance, loving forgiveness, and strength to cope during such times.

When the clouds roll in, they sometimes stay for days, especially when the disappointment is experienced by those we love. Yet God's abiding love helps us to see the sunshine . . . even on the gloomiest days.

10
The Prize Gift

"It is more blessed to give than to receive."

—Acts 20:35

The warm June day was perfect for my annual garage sale. The sky welcomed the morning with a brilliant blue, and the tall pine trees seemed cleaner and greener than ever after the brief shower at daybreak. The Florida sun's rays were enough to let you know that summer was here without being overly intense, and even the birds seemed to chirp in an inviting tone. Yes, it was the perfect day.

I always wait until June to hold this annual garage sale. In fact, I always wait until a few days before the family vacation. The money we make at my garage sale has always gone for those unexpected extras on vacation—another movie or two, a special unplanned dinner out, T-shirts from an amusement park or a scenic attraction.

Getting ready for this sale has always been a family affair. The kids go through their dresser drawers, closets, and shelves and supply the sale with items that are too small, too babyish, or too boring. They set up their table at the sale and keep the profits for their unexpected extras on vacation. My husband Bob and I work for weeks going through the stacks of books, boxes, and unwanted items stored all year in the dusty attic. We forage through our closets, our work desks, the kitchen, and the garage and make a pact that if an item has not been used in the past two years, it goes.

A few days before the sale, the family makes bright poster-sized signs and places them around the neighborhood. We call the radio stations and even place a classified advertisement in the local paper. We certainly get ready for our annual event, and we want to make sure everyone knows.

The night before the big sale is definitely a "family night." The entire clan sets up the garage for the next day, folds clothes, prices items, and tries to make attractive the many neglected objects begging for a new owner.

This year was different. Usually the annual sale was filled with clothing, small trinkets, and odds and ends that we never found use for. But this year I had an item that would certainly bring in a lot of money. We had redecorated our youngest daughter's room in the spring, and we were going to sell her entire bedroom furniture, including bunk beds, a dresser, spreads, pillows, curtains, and an area rug. I had advertised this item as a true prize and could hardly wait to see how much it would bring. Certainly enough to have extra fun on our vacation without worrying about staying within our budget.

"Mom, people are already lined up outside the garage," my oldest, Rob, yelled to me while I was fixing breakfast the morning of the sale.

I bolted out the kitchen door and pressed the garage door button only to see legs of all sizes revealed as the door crept up.

"Are you open yet?"

"Can we just look around?"

"Do you mind if we wait in your driveway?"

The eager voices of the first shoppers urged me to end my duty as cook and begin my role as clerk.

"Certainly, we'll open a bit early. Come on and shop," I told the strangers enthusiastically while wiping my hands on my apron. "There are many bargains on the tables, and we have a special price on the bedroom suite that is by the back wall."

I motioned to the people to look over my prize item for sale. After all, selling the bedroom suite was going to make our vacation one to remember.

The early birds bought several items from the tables; two women were interested in the bedroom suite.

"Would you come down in your price on the furniture?" one woman asked as she tried to negotiate a deal.

"Definitely not now," I replied cheerfully. I was going to hold on to that gem until later. My price was fair, and I wanted to make the most money I could for our vacation.

"Well," the woman said. "My name is Mrs. Stevens. Take my name and number. If you don't get what you want for it by the end of the day, please give me the opportunity to purchase it for a bit less. It would be perfect in the new addition we are adding to our home."

I wrote down her name and number and kept it safe in the cash box next to me. I patted the cash box as I closed the lid. Yes, this sale would certainly be successful.

People came in droves to the sale during the morning hours. The June temperature rose with the sun. The garage, filled with goods, seemed smaller than ever with the sticky bodies of customers moving among the tables of sale items.

I stopped periodically throughout the morning to go inside to count the money we had earned and put the larger bills away.

". . . 85, 90, 100," I counted slowly to myself. *That's not too bad for a few hours,* I thought. But just wait until I sell that furniture. That will triple my profits. Our vacation would certainly be exciting.

Then it happened. I walked out into the garage and saw my husband talking with a young couple near the furniture. The slim woman was very pregnant and was holding the hands of twin girls who appeared to be about four years old. The young man by her side had his arm in a cast and was holding the hand of another child, a boy about seven years old.

Perfect. The perfect customer for my special furniture. I just knew these people would want such a deal to use for their growing family.

"Deb, come over here." Bob motioned for me to come talk to the young couple.

"This is my wife Debbie," he said, "and this is Virginia and Ted Davis."

"Nice to meet you. Are you new in the neighborhood?"

"Oh, no," Virginia smiled as she spoke. Her face seemed tired and drawn to be such a young woman. I will never forget how her eyes were filled with hurt and pain. "We live two miles away in that new subdivision by the air station, or should I say we used to live two miles away."

"Deb, you might remember reading about Ted and Virginia in the paper last weekend," Bob said. "Their home was vandalized while they were away visiting relatives. Everything they owned—furniture, clothing, dishes, appliances—was either stolen or broken. When they got back home last Sunday night, they walked into a nightmare."

"The police still have no leads on what happened," Ted added matter-of-factly. "It has been an unbelievable experience. The children lost all their toys, even my son's bike was broken to pieces. I fractured my arm while trying to clean up some of the mess, so I'm off work until next week, and Virginia is due to go into labor anytime. We have been told that the insurance money will come in to cover some of the items. But it won't be nearly enough." The man's voice seemed to accept the adversity, but you could tell he was being strong for the family.

I did recall reading of the tragedy in the paper the weekend before and thinking how sad it was that this had happened to these people. Who in his right mind would think of doing such a violent, destructive act? I remember thinking how close this vandalism was to our neighborhood and that it could easily have happened to us.

"We are out looking for items to try to set up our home again as quickly as possible," Virginia said quietly as she rubbed her large protruding belly. "A local church down the street gave us a bed for the master bedroom, but the kids have been sleeping on blankets in their rooms all week."

"Is this the lowest price you would take on this bedroom set?" Ted asked slowly.

I looked at the young couple and their precious children. It seemed that all eyes were staring back at me, innocent eyes that were pained by a criminal's act.

"Uh, well . . ." I stammered as I thought about a price. "Bob, could we talk in the kitchen for a minute?"

Closing the door behind us, I said, "Bob, you know we can't charge them anything for the furniture. How can I make a profit off of people whose lives have been so devastated?"

"Well, what do you want to do?" he asked. "You would be giving up several hundred dollars you had planned on."

No, I thought to myself. *I hadn't planned on this money. This money was always extra.* We would still get our vacation, but more importantly, would this family get their lives back together?

I made up my mind quickly.

"Free? You mean just take it?" Ted's eyes lit up with a bit of life as he spoke.

"Oh, yes, and I have a stack of dishes and bowls on that table out front that you could use until you get new ones," I said with tears in my eyes.

"Maybe your girls could wear some of the clothes on that other table," my fifteen-year-old daughter who had been standing with us added. "And Ashley has a bunch of puzzles, dolls, and books on her table."

"Listen, I know that if more people knew of what had happened to you, they would be more than willing to help get you through this," Bob said. "I'll tell our church secretary on Monday morning to list items you need in the church newsletter. I know our congregation will respond."

Virginia had tears running down her face as she hugged the two small girls. "We never expected anything to be given to us like this. We're not members of your church. We don't even live in your neighborhood."

"That's what we're here for," Bob said as he hugged the young couple. "Now let me back up my van, and I'll get my son to help us load up what you can use."

The garage sale ended shortly after the Davis family left. A sudden thunderstorm forced the shoppers to run to the safety of their cars. We closed the garage door with no one waiting to shop.

Later that evening the phone rang.

"Mrs. Stevens?" I questioned my son. "I don't know a Mrs. Stevens?"

"She said she wanted to buy that furniture earlier today and wondered if it was still for sale."

"Oh, that." I laughed aloud as I thought about my terrific prize which was going to make our vacation the best ever.

"Tell Mrs. Stevens that I decided not to sell it after all because it was a gift."

Yes, the furniture was a gift, a gift to a young family who needed and deserved it.

Jesus taught us that it is more blessed to give than to receive.

The Christian life is full of gifts, for us and for others. Giving my prized item showed me the true rewards of reaching out to those in need.

As I turned the light off that night and got into my clean bed, I felt warm and contented, knowing that two small girls were also getting into a bed after having slept on the floor for almost a week. This was going to be the best vacation ever!

11

Helping Children Share Their Faith

"I pray that you may be active in sharing your faith."

—Philemon 6

When I asked my daughter what her Sunday school lesson was about last week, she bubbled with enthusiasm.

"Mrs. Seay talked about faith," Ashley said with confidence. "She told us that when we really experience God's love in our lives, we will receive a personal faith. And at the end of class, she asked each of us to share our faith with a friend this week."

I have to confess that I was caught off-guard by young Ashley's new enthusiasm for sharing her faith. Was this the same child who had shunned family devotions the week before? Nonetheless, I was pleased that someone had opened her eyes to the possibilities of a personal relationship with Jesus Christ.

Can a personal faith be enthusiastically explained in the family so our children are challenged with personal witnessing and the desire to tell others the Good News?

Faith means commitment, trust, and caring for others. Faith enables us to risk sharing our lives with others in meaningful relationships. Because of faith that is nurtured in a caring Christian home, new lives are constantly being changed. Faith in a living Lord gives empty, lonely lives new meaning and purpose.

Faith is an ongoing process. Theologians realize that just as people mature and grow in stages, so our faith develops in stages. Religious educators have found that just as a baby crawls before he walks and develops physically and mentally in sequence, so our faith in God begins and then increases as we mature spiritually.

In the book *Will Our Children Have Faith?* (New York: The Seabury Press, 1976, 91–99) author John Westerhoff III suggests four stages of faith development.

1. Experienced Faith. This experience-oriented stage is highlighted by action and reaction to others and events. That is, in this beginning stage, a person believes only what is experienced, observing and copying other people.

2. Affiliative Faith. At this stage, a person moves into affiliating with significant persons and events. Affiliative faith involves belonging (such as to a group), participation, and a feeling of being a part of something important.

3. Searching Faith. A person begins to use the mind to make critical judgments, including questioning and doubting, and to experiment with alternative courses of action.

4. Owned Faith. This is the ultimate ideal. Faith is truly "owned." A person begins to feel the need to witness, to behave with an integrity that supports personal belief.

Has your child developed an experienced, affiliative, searching, or owned faith? It is important for you as a parent to provide biblical information along with personal experience so your child's ultimate response can be that of an owned faith and a personal witness to others.

It seems ironic that many Christians don't seem to make the correlation between their faith and such things as their work, their family relationships, or their approach to decision making or politics. Because these Christians are hesitant to talk about their faith, they maintain a relationship with God that could be labeled a "private faith." According to this report, Christians with a private faith usually don't know how to "go public" in either words or actions, even if they wanted to.

What about your child? Is your child comfortable going public with his faith? Does he seem to find joy in those special moments where he can talk about God's love in his own life?

Think back to your childhood days. Do you remember the first Christian who had a tremendous influence in your life? This person was probably someone who made you feel loved, who made you want to learn what they knew, and who brought out the best in you.

What did this Christian do that made such an impression on your life? Was it his attitude toward you? Did this special person believe in you? affirm you? care for you? encourage you? It is amazing how many of these descriptions of the first Christians who touched our lives look like an accurate depiction of the incarnate love of Christ!

Thank God that someone cared enough to share the incarnate love of Christ with us! A Christian witness who shares this "owned faith" publicly combines actions and words as he or she lets the love of Christ move through him into the life of the other.

Personal evangelism through telling of the faith is often trying. Some introverted people struggle just thinking about sharing their faith. Even the most gregarious Christian may become tongue-tied when asked to share his faith, much less anything else so personal. My teenage son confided: "I'm so afraid that if I tell someone about my relationship with God he will ask me a question about the Bible that I don't know; then I really won't be an effective witness. Besides that, I would be totally embarrassed."

Personal evangelism and witnessing is part of living a Christian life! In Acts 1:8, Jesus spoke clearly about witnessing, saying, "You will receive power when the Holy Spirit comes on you; and you will be my witnesses." And in 2 Corinthians 5:20, we read, "We are Christ's ambassadors, as though God were making his appeal through us."

We need to convey to our children that they may be the best Christian someone else knows. In fact, they may be the only Christian another person knows! Realizing this, it seems all the more vital that our children learn to share the peace and joy that Christ brings to our lives.

Ask your children where they would be right now if someone had not witnessed about the Christian faith. Would they still believe in Christ? We know how important it is for people to share their faith. Now the challenge is ours to continue the 2,000-year-old legacy of the Christian faith by sharing it with others.

Know Yourself

Through prayer and meditation, we can realize a more personal faith with God through Jesus Christ. This knowledge of self is vital in order to share a faith that has truly touched our souls. Prayer continues the ongoing personal relationship between God and self. Times of meditation and aloneness with God allow you to learn who you are and *whose* you are.

Attend Church Regularly

Encourage your children to know their church. One of the best witnessing opportunities we can have is to invite someone to our church where programs, classes, and prayer groups can meet his or her spiritual needs. Find out what is available at your church—studies, small groups, children's choirs, youth meetings, women's groups, men's studies. Share this information with your children. Just as a good retailer must know his product in order to sell it, a good Christian must know his church and the learning experiences that are offered in order to witness effectively.

Study the Bible

It is important for a good witness to be in study—privately and with others. The Bible offers inspiration, strength, knowledge, and insight into human living and can give a strong background to every Christian who is striving for an "owned" faith.

Share Your Faith

My children have asked, "What exactly do I say when I have an opportunity to tell someone about Jesus?" You simply tell others what you believe—this is the best way to explain the gospel to others. You don't have to *preach* or memorize passages from the Bible. Relate your Christian experience to others simply by telling what you have experienced. I overheard Ashley sharing her faith with a friend whose grandmother was ill. She simply said, "I know Jesus will take care of her. He loves us all." Those simple words spoken in a child's language were a powerful testimony of her faith.

Encourage your children to begin to share their faith at home, with their grandparents, in their Sunday school class, or in any "safe" environment with people they know.

Let your children know that when they share their faith, people will ask questions. Just as they prepared in school for exams, children can prepare for witnessing by anticipating questions and finding answers.

Not only must our children know what they believe, but they must also continually seek ways of verbalizing their faith to others until this personal faith becomes truly owned, a part of their Christian life-style. They must trust God for courage and strength, risk that the time is right, and take action when the opportunity to share their relationship with God through Jesus Christ presents itself.

Jesus' final emphasis in His ministry is to "Go and make disciples . . . teaching them to obey" (Matthew 28:19–20). Obeying this commandment begins with our personal witness in the home as we teach our children the sharing of information and the art of the gracious confrontation—providing that special environment where grace can be experienced and an owned faith can be the expected result.

12

When a Morning Lark Marries a Night Owl

"My perfect one is unique."

—Song of Solomon 6:9

I had always believed the adage "Birds of a feather flock together." But when my husband and I married and combined our two opposite body clocks, I ignored this saying. After all, many marriages had worked with greater differences than we had.

According to some recent marriage surveys, our eighteen-year marriage just can't possibly be working. Marriages where one person likes to stay up late and the other person retires early and gets up early are just not compatible, this study said. This report also stated that in these marriages there wasn't enough time for private conversation, the communication that should take place in a marriage was stilted, and the two different body clocks created inharmonious rhythms.

I don't like to dispute the experts, but I would have if they had included me in their survey. So can a morning lark really be happily married to a night owl? Indeed! Let me give you an example of how our body clocks find harmony.

It is 5 A.M. My eyes pop wide open without the assistance of an alarm. It is another gorgeous day and there is so much to do. I hear my husband breathing deeply as he sleeps next to me. Quietly I get up and tiptoe out of the bedroom. The birds chirping at daybreak add a cheerful sound as I pour my coffee. This is "my time." Two hours—I have two wonderful hours to read, pray, write, and think clearly before anyone else awakens. The early bird hours are the time in my day that I spend alone with God. As I unload the dishwasher, make school lunches, dust a table or two, and fold last night's laundry, I am constantly thinking of ideas, stopping to make a list or two, and asking God to give direction to the day.

As delightful as this time is, all good things come to an end. About three o'clock each afternoon, my body, begins to tire. My mind becomes a bit foggy, and the great, creative ideas are less frequent. I put all big projects on hold for the day and begin to focus on family duties—kids home from school, carpools to run, a last-minute errand, dinner to cook, dishes to clean, and homework to monitor.

Let's turn back the clock to see how Bob, the night owl, approaches the day.

The alarm rings for three loud minutes before my sleepy husband finally turns it off. Seven in the morning. It seems like the middle of the night to this devoted night owl, but seeing the daylight pouring in his window he knows it is a reality. Bob stumbles out of bed, bumps into a wall or two, and finally turns on the shower to help signal his body to wake up.

Family members are greeted with a soft, "Good morning, Deb," and "Can you turn the radios down, kids?" Breakfast is eaten while reading the paper, not too much conversation yet. A quick kiss and his blurry eyes guide him to the car. Another day has begun.

Bob spends his early mornings at the office in study, then begins to see parishioners after 9:30 A.M., once his body has realized the owner really did wake it up.

Here is where our differences begin. By 9:30 A.M., I have already edited several manuscripts, written an outline or two for articles, vacuumed the bedrooms, wiped down the bathrooms, and started early dinner preparations. *Where did my day go,* I wonder as I pause for a refreshing glass of iced tea. By 9:30 A.M. my husband has settled into his office and has started to open his mail from the previous day. *My day is just beginning,* he thinks as he pours his first cup of coffee.

By 3:00 in the afternoon I am almost through with my day.

But Bob has just finished a luncheon meeting and is starting his afternoon schedule.

At 7:30 P.M. Bob and I pause to be together—alone. As the children work in their rooms, we sit in the den and talk about our respective days. My mind is through being creative, so I can think about his needs and his dreams. His mind has not fully clicked into the creative mode, so he can think about my needs and dreams. We talk about children and family and bills and vacation. We argue about politics and current events and teenage curfews and the neighbor's barking dog. We hug and kiss and smile and laugh. We joke and cry and pray and sit in solitude. Yes, we are compatible.

It is 9:30 P.M. The children have been tucked in, and their lights are out. I'm ready for bed too. My mind is tired, my body aches, and the cool covers look inviting. As I turn off my light by the bed, my husband kisses me goodnight and tiptoes back into the den.

Now, let the good times roll. This is Bob's time. He thinks and creates. He plans and reads. He makes prayer lists, job lists, and visitation lists. He tinkers with a new program on the computer, throws in a load of wash, watches the news, and listens to the new CD. He quietly plays the piano in the distant living room, hums the verse to a new hymn, and prays aloud. He is alive, vibrant, creative, and very awake.

The mantle clock strikes midnight, and Bob reminds his body that it has to be tired. Finally, his day is done as he turns back the bedcovers and crawls in.

Perhaps it is our strong independence that keeps our marriage together. After all, if we had the same body clock, we might not have those times for aloneness and creative thinking. I often think people who in some ways are different from each other can fill voids in each other's lives. My cheerfulness during the morning hours gets the family off the ground and moving. Bob's energy at night helps complete our busy day when the family's needs change.

Rather than a study by modern science, I claim the Scripture verse "Where two or three come together in my name, there am I with them" (Matthew 18:20). His love is the basis for our relationship.

Our marriage is living proof that the morning lark and the

night owl can flock together, even if these two old birds do differ in some ways. We have experienced that with a common belief in Jesus Christ, along with some open communication, planning of daily schedules, and allowing each other to find personal time, our marriage can be sound and fulfilling.

13
See the Possibility

"Let us not become weary in doing good, for at the proper time we will reap a harvest if we do not give up."

—Galatians 6:9

"I think I would enjoy parenting a lot more if there was no such thing as stages in my child's development." My friend Lori made this remark over coffee one morning after experiencing a trying week with her fourth-grade daughter. "It's so easy to love Jenni when she toes the line, but when she starts asserting herself and rebelling, I really find it hard to even like her, much less love her."

I was able to identify with her. Raising three children, I know the difficulty of loving that "unlovely" child. In our family there always seems to be a child in some stage. Of course, the child in the stage always seems to pick that moment when you are under other stresses and not quite ready to deal with unlovely behavior. And just as soon as that child matures and moves past this stage in development, the next child in line seems to fall in.

Remember when your child was just a baby? Wasn't it easy to sit and cuddle? Even when the baby cried to be fed or changed, there was always something about the innocence of its helplessness that compelled you to hug and kiss it.

What about your child as she grows and develops? Is it still easy to hug that rebellious fifth grader who is about to enter puberty? Or what about the third-grade boy who is expressing himself in a "new" language? Or even the precious first grader who flatly refuses to pick up her room?

No, it isn't always easy to love the unlovely. Finding the good qualities in a child who is in a difficult period in life is trying, even for the most patient parent. As Christians we have the commandment from Jesus to care especially for the unlovely and to reach out in compassion to those in need.

Jesus teaches us that "Whatever you did for one of the least of these brothers of mine, you did for me" (Matthew 25:40). If we cannot accept our children even at their unlovely moments then perhaps we need to work on our relationship with our Lord.

There are many virtues the Bible describes when it comes to living the full Christian life. These virtues need to be discovered and used enthusiastically, especially when unlovely children tempt our patience. Perhaps the following suggestions can pull you through trying moments in your life.

Have Patience

The challenge of Hebrews 12:1 is this: "Let us run with perseverance the race marked out for us." This perseverance involves not giving up in times of crisis, but hanging on and accepting the situation until changes occur.

When our middle child entered fifth grade, we were not ready for the changes that were occurring in her life. Puberty? Why that was several years away. Wrong! She experienced changes in her life that most girls experience in seventh and eighth grade, and we experienced the rebellious and challenging behavior that goes along with entering the adolescent years.

"But she is just a child," I complained to her pediatrician. "She is only in elementary school and she is already five feet four inches tall."

"These times will be trying, I know," the doctor said with empathy. "And they may be more difficult for her because she is the first in her crowd to mature. But be patient, this too will pass."

We were patient. Yes, we did have to go to our room and close the door many evenings when unlovely behavior was displayed. And we gave many hugs—hugs that were difficult to give at times.

But now Brittnye is in high school and is a most settled young lady. We had many unlovely moments for two years, but the caring young woman she is now was worth the trials.

The Lord's time is not always our time. Often we adopt the attitude, "I want it and I want it now." Our Lord reminds us of the virtue of patience and asks us to wait upon Him.

Be Persistent

In Acts 2:42 Paul offers more strength for being steadfast: "They devoted themselves to the apostles' teaching and to the fellowship, to the breaking of bread and to prayer."

As a parent, you can help your troubled child feel stability by demonstrating a deep commitment. Such persistence motivates family members to believe in a power that moves deeper than the surface love of family. This commitment to the child keeps the relationship strong, even when the enthusiasm is low. Persistence involves loyalty to the child's potential instead of to the behavior you might see at a bad moment.

When my friend Sharon adopted her first son, the agency told her not to have "great expectations" because of the poor prenatal care of his birth mother. Sharon, a stubborn young woman, refused to listen.

"Jake is in the third grade and is excelling," she told me at the open house at school. "He isn't easy to raise, but I am determined to help him be all he can be. I see the potential in this child, and I am going to develop it all I can."

Be in Prayer

The psalmist says, "Every morning and noon I cry out in distress, and he hears my voice" (Psalm 55:17).

Prayer does change things! In a broken relationship in your family, prayer can help to unite the members and can give purpose to the problem at hand.

Parents who experience crisis in the family because of a child with a strong will or emotional problems contend that prayer is the one strength they lean on.

"Prayer seemed to bring peace to even the most horrendous moment with Jason," a father spoke. "After getting upset with him for losing his bike or for failing his test, I had to pray or I felt I would really lose my temper. You know, the power of prayer helped change me as much as it helped change him."

Prayer can be that special communication that enables a difficult child to know of God's love and power, even when the enthusiasm is not felt. Prayer can also be the peace a distraught parent needs during moments of anguish.

See the Possibility

In Mark 14:36, Jesus prayed, "Abba, Father . . . everything is possible for you. Take this cup from me. Yet not what I will, but what you will." Paul teaches in Philippians 4:13, "I can do everything through him who gives me strength."

Our Christian faith is a faith of hope. Realizing the possibility and promise in the difficult child is one of the keys to successful Christian living.

"When all others turned away from Shelly, I hung in—as difficult as it was," a mother said at a support group in our church. "Shelly was so bright, but she was also very opinionated and strong-willed. That is an awesome combination for a child, especially for a teacher to deal with."

"Finally, when Shelly hit high school, something clicked," the woman continued. "She got involved in student government and was elected president of her school. Kids that used to make fun of her in elementary school now respect her and look up to her. Her intelligence and will were channeled into leadership."

Seeing the possibility in your child during unlovely moments can be exciting. But this awesome power of God can be seen only if you have an attitude of anticipation.

Have you had moments when your child was difficult to love? Remember the promise of the Scripture passage found in Job 14:7: "At least there is hope for a tree: If it is cut down, it will sprout again, and its new shoots will not fail." Knowing there is the promise of hope even in seemingly hopeless situations can make the difference in changing lives. And you, the Christian parent, can help make this difference.

14

Correcting the Golden Rule

"I tell you the truth, whatever you did for one of the least of these brothers of mine, you did for me."
—Matthew 25:40

"Who cares" is a common phrase among children. But I was shocked when I overheard my son yell "Who cares" (which being interpreted meant, "So what!") to his younger sister after she told him of a birthday party invitation she had received. Among adults in today's world, however, I think the words "who cares" may be a genuine question, as they wonder if anyone has empathy for them in what they face.

Developing caring qualities in a child takes years of patience and nurturing; the rewards are not seen for years, when the child's "who cares" attitude becomes like that of Christ: "I care."

Caring is a learned trait, not an instinct. A child who is spoken to in a loving manner, who is given limits for his behavior, and who is part of a family where genuine caring is shown is more likely to develop such attributes as patience, kindness, and consideration.

You may need to evaluate the time spent with your child. Recently, I spent my entire day with my three children, but I was answering them with phrases such as "Please leave me alone right now," and "I'll answer that later." I found myself so absorbed in doing things for my children that I was neglecting the interaction needed to build my relationship with each one.

Planning to spend quality time with each child is vital in order to establish caring. This individual time could be one hour during the day—after school, early in the morning, or before bedtime. This one hour, if truly dedicated to that child, is more important than many hours spent there just being with him. During this time relate to him personally: Talk about your own childhood. Listen to your child's fears and frustrations. Help him feel secure in your love for him.

Verbalize your feelings with your child. If a situation occurs in which the child behaves in a way that shows a lack of caring, help the child put himself on the receiving end of such treatment. How would he feel if that happened to him? What considerations would he like shown toward him? By helping the child understand his feelings—his own likes and dislikes—you may help him become more loving to those around him.

Explain to your child why you do caring things for others. If you take a neighbor flowers or food during an illness, let your child know you did it because you care for that person.

Let your child know your feelings when someone makes you feel special, or upsets you. Help your child realize that people can contribute to helping others through caring ways, such as being considerate and helpful.

Teach your children the Golden Rule: "Do to others as you would have them do to you" (Luke 6:31). Role play situations where this rule can be used. I recognized the need of such an approach after interrupting my three children in the middle of a spat. When I asked why they were acting so rowdy, my youngest child replied, "We were just doing the Golden Rule. You do to others what they do to you!" Developing caring concepts takes time, explanations, and maturity!

Be considerate of your child's feelings. Don't compare him or his abilities to others. Many parents are guilty of thoughtlessly remarking, "Why can't you make good grades like Sharon does?" or "Can you talk softly like Jason does?" This comparison only destroys the self-image necessary for confident, caring living.

Realize that your child is unique and fits into God's plan for being special. Help him find his unique gifts and talents and build them up to him and others. For example, if your child is helpful during the day, tell the family about it. If the child brings home a report or picture from school, take time to discuss it and comment on the attributes the child expressed, such as patience in drawing, research, neatness, or printing.

A child learns caring mainly through watching the way you act toward others. If you are inconsistent in showing concern for others, expect your child to be inconsistent also. If you have a lot of anger, frustrations, and other negative emotions, your child will also. On the other hand, if you demonstrate love and caring to others, your child will probably pick them up. How you handle neighbor relationships, family matters, and community situations reinforces priorities that you have spoken of as being important in your own life.

I watched my daughter pick a handful of daisies as she walked up the drive one day. As she handed me the wilted stems, she said enthusiastically, "Mom, I've had a wonderful day." Her enthusiasm and love for living was so complete she wanted to share it with others. This giving and selfless love is in part a learned response taught by caring parents, teachers, and other important people in her life.

Discipline and firmness also are evidence of caring. We have all experienced how children, and even adults, exhibit negative forms of behavior to get attention. Often the child who is a behavior problem feels a need for love and comfort. Allowing a child to control you and others around him only adds to his insecurity. Deal with behavior problems. Help him understand that you are disciplining because you care; you are punishing him because of your love for him. It is often difficult for a child to understand the limits and consequences of his behavior. Yet if the parent is consistent with discipline, a child will sense the caring and concern.

Teaching a child to care for those around him is not a simple task. Caring is a learned process developed through interaction with loving caregivers who take time to be with the child, talk with the child, and even say no at times. A child will remember the moments when you demonstrated care and concern as you teach him how to act in Christian love.

15
A Guide for Kingdom Living

"[Jesus] began to teach them, saying: 'Blessed are the poor in spirit, for theirs is the kingdom of heaven.'"

—Matthew 5:2–3

No one ever said that parenting would be easy. As our three children express their ideas and viewpoints in totally unconventional ways, we wonder if we ever acted that way. Did we really try to do our "own thing" years ago?

As parents, we must constantly evaluate our life-style, for we are important and highly visible role models to our children. If we do nothing else, we must set high examples for our young. Periodically we must ask ourselves: Is God my partner in life? Is the way I live, in agreement with Christ's teachings? Is my relationship with my child honest, open, and accepting?

We must recognize and acknowledge that parents have room for growth and change. As we study the Scriptures, we can begin to identify our own strengths and weaknesses. Then as we evaluate our own life-style, we can seek to change our weaknesses and increase our strengths.

The Bible is full of inspiration and messages that will meet us where we are in our lives. In Matthew 5:3–10, Christ gives us eight keys to the kingdom of God—a kingdom that is also for us today.

Blessed Are the Poor in Spirit

Are you honest with your child? Or do you claim to have all the answers? To be "poor in spirit" involves admitting to the child that you do not have all the answers to life. By admitting this weakness, strength is gained as together the parent and child can turn to God for answers and guidance.

Most parents, most adults for that matter, have a real fear of admitting that they have need of help or outside strength. One father at a recent parenting seminar told me, "What would my son think of me if he heard that I lost my position at work? He would lose faith in me."

As a parent genuinely relates to the youth and is open and honest, the youth will see the parent in a different light—as a true human being.

A close friend of the family sat down with her two older children and explained that the family was having financial difficulties and that they would have to struggle to tighten the budget. As she exposed her vulnerability to her children, they accepted their mother as a real person and sought creative ways to pitch in and work together.

To be "poor in spirit" does not bring about feelings of despair and anguish. Rather, this poverty is full of reward and fulfillment as lives are made whole.

Blessed Are Those Who Mourn

Remember how it felt to sit home alone on the weekends while everyone else was at the school party? Remember how it felt to be chosen last for the kick-ball game? to have your best friend move away? to break up with your steady date? to experience rejection for the first time? *Oh, kid's stuff,* you might say. But to your child, these hurts and disappointments are just as real as the rejection you experience as an adult.

Listen to your child as he expresses his sorrows, and avoid judging him for his feelings of anger and resentment. Being a caring parent who is willing to listen sympathetically is one more step toward building a satisfying parent-child relationship.

A mother of a preteen said, "I am basically a shy person. I like to keep my inner thoughts to myself, but I am learning to share my past experiences with my daughter. Just the other day I told her about the time when I was her age and I thought I'd never grow any taller. My complexion was so bad that I felt it would never clear up. As I openly talked to her about my past as an early adolescent, she seemed to relax and identify with me. She began to accept her mixed emotions and feelings as being normal and felt free to move on to another stage of development."

When your child is feeling low, give the hope of the Christian faith to fill the empty moments. Suggestions to pray, to study the Bible, to meditate about God, and to listen for Him in others will enable your child to find fulfillment in times of aloneness.

Blessed Are the Meek

Who is in control? Do you allow God to be your partner? Often it is much easier and more natural to want to have control, be in charge. Yet as we allow God to use us through our strengths and weaknesses, we can feel the inner peace He gives.

"Does God use kids too?" a child asked in my Sunday school class. Oh, yes! Yet in the midst of the enthusiasm and energy that accompanies youth, it is often harder for children to realize this.

By being a dedicated role model and example, how you wait on God for guidance can be seen by your child. The awareness of Christian meekness comes alive as the child sees you accepting God's control.

Blessed Are Those Who Hunger and Thirst for Righteousness

Do you radiate a living faith? By including in your daily routine a time for Bible study and prayer, you can strive for a deeper experience with God. By being actively involved in your local church, in worship, in Sunday school, and on committees, you can understand your faith more accurately. By encouraging your child to be active in Christian fellowship groups, Sunday school, and services at your church, you are continuing the foundation you began at his birth.

Discuss your faith openly with your children. Use your knowledge and training to help guide their lives. This involves thanking God for the good times as well as seeking comfort and guidance during the crises.

Blessed Are the Merciful

Caring and showing mercy go hand in hand. What does caring involve? Genuine caring for our children involves loving them enough to teach them, by degrees, to make decisions, to enable them to become independent, to let go. Caring also means saying no or administering restrictions when rules or limits are broken.

A father of three teenagers said, "God has given us a wealth of resources to draw from to show His mercy: Understanding, compassion, empathy, and patience are just a few. I feel it is important to communicate our continual care to our children so they see that our faith is more than just idle talk. When God's selfless love is reflected, the child can respond with his own decision for Christ."

Blessed Are the Pure in Heart

What kind of role model are you for your children? Are you approachable? That is, is your life genuine and real enough so that your child feels comfort in confiding in you?

People build barriers around themselves as they pretend to be what they are not. These barriers inhibit communication between parent and child. To avoid this, you can "risk" exposing your inner self to your child. This means talking about your fears, hopes, failures, and dreams. As you let your child hear or see how you've solved a problem, conquered a fear, or met a goal, he can experience part of the openness and freedom the Christian faith gives.

Blessed Are the Peacemakers

Jesus Christ was a peacemaker, not just a peace keeper. How do you deal with conflict in your own family? Do you go that extra mile for something you know is right and good? Or do you merely brush aside the truth, hoping to avoid conflict?

Standing with your child, believing in his worth as a Christian young person, and being fair with those around you are ways of reflecting this peace.

A youth Sunday school teacher told of how she dealt with conflict with older elementary children. "When conflict arises among the children, I try to listen to all sides of the story and avoid taking sides while striving for a fair compromise. This manner of dealing with conflict helps justice to occur in the situation without ignoring the truth."

This manner of dealing with conflict works in families as well. Acceptance and love are shown as caring parents encourage peaceful family situations.

Blessed Are Those Who Are Persecuted for Righteousness Sake

Do you really know what you believe? Can you verbalize your beliefs? Do you put your faith into action? Sharing your faith through words and actions is vital for the Christian. Often, especially during the teen years, doubts occur as the young person seeks to define his own faith and beliefs. It is imperative when this doubting occurs that the parent consistently help the teen find answers. This involves encouraging Bible study, sharing your personal faith story, and asking others such as the pastor or a teacher to encourage the seeker.

When a faith issue is challenged, avoid arguing the question. Few are won into the Kingdom through arguments. Do not compromise your beliefs; just continue to love the other person.

God's Word gives us life-changing guidelines for happiness and fulfillment. As we minister to our children by being genuine, open, caring, and sharing our personal faith, we can truly experience God's kingdom in our lives even (and especially!) during their childhood.

16

Hope in a Cemetery

"For God so loved the world that he gave his one and only Son, that whoever believes in him shall not perish but have eternal life."

—John 3:16

A visit years ago to my brother's home in the mountains of North Georgia provided a new adventure for my three children. My brother pastored a historic red brick church that towered over a grassy hill beside his home. Across the street in the large church graveyard is where our adventure began.

"Hey, what are those tall, white rocks across the street?" Ashley asked as we drove up to the home that evening. "Wow! One of the rocks even glows in the dark."

When the car halted, both back doors flew open and our three children raced through the tall grass to the cemetery.

"What is this place? What are these rocks for? Why are some rocks larger than others?" Brittnye's questions were endless. Realizing that a cemetery could provide a valuable experience, we halted the inquisitions and planned to spend the following morning exploring in the graveyard.

The next day the three children, my husband, and I explored the old cemetery.

"Hey, read the gravestones, Mom," Rob, my oldest, yelled. "This one says 1802."

We brushed the encrusted dirt off the front of the tombstone but could barely make out the inscription.

"Why does it just say 'Jones?'" Brittnye asked with amazement. "Didn't Jones have a first and middle name?"

I laughed at their concerns, but then realized these questions were serious. I replied, "I am sure he did, but perhaps they didn't put first names on tombstones in those days."

Brittnye then brushed off the dirt and mold on the accompanying stone. "This one just says 'Jones' wife,'" she said as she giggled. "I know she had a name, Mommy."

We moved on to look further up the hill. I could tell the excitement of exploring the old cemetery had turned to concern for the two children.

"Why are there so many little tombstones?" Brittnye asked. "They have only one number on them."

I explained how those were the markers for little babies who never lived. "They probably died at birth or when they were just a few days old," I said gently. I then explained to the children about the poor health care one hundred years ago. "Doctors just couldn't treat some babies. Some children in these mountains were born at home," I said sympathetically. "Some never had a chance."

"Well, when I grow up I'll learn to be a pediatrician and help all of these poor, little babies." Brittnye confidently made a young child's pledge to help mankind.

"Hey," Rob yelled from the bottom of the hill. "It's kinda scary around here. I'm heading back to Uncle Mac's house."

"Wait Rob," I called. "Let's talk for a minute first."

I gathered the family up in a close circle around the old shade tree at the top of the hill and began to ask the children questions. "What do you think death is like? Do you see it as punishment? What feelings do you have about it?"

Brittnye was the first to speak. "I guess it's sorta like going to sleep," she said confidently. "You just close your eyes and sleep until God takes you to be with Him."

"Well, it is similar to that, Britt," I replied, "except that when you sleep, you wake up. When you die, you don't wake up the same as you always had." I thought about the prayer she had worried about as a preschooler— "If I should die before I wake"—and how frightened she had been that she might not wake up the next morning.

"Yeah," Rob added, holding up a small roly-poly bug. "It's just like this bug. He is just plain dead. Look, he doesn't even kick."

Brittnye grabbed the bug and tried to toss it about in her hand to give it life. But the bug was dead and no amount of stimulation could make him come back to life.

"Well, probably just bad people die, Mommy," Brittnye said softly. "I still worry about those babies."

"Brittnye," I held her close to me as I spoke, "death is a part of God's plan. Just as life is. We will all die someday. When? Only God knows that."

"Well, when I die I don't want to be stuck in the ground with a glow-in-the-dark rock on top of me." Rob's braveness was slowly decreasing. "I thought I got to be with Jesus."

"That is the beauty of being a Christian, son!" I said as I grinned and hugged both children. It was a beautiful moment to interject the hope of our Christian faith. "Your body may be placed in the cemetery. The tombstone may be placed at the site for people to remember you. But the most important thing is that your spirit—the real you—will go on to be with our Heavenly Father."

"Oh, Mommy, you sound like a preacher!" Brittnye teased.

I laughed. "Don't you see how a cemetery can be a happy place? Look at this tombstone." I pointed to a marker that had musical notes carved all over it. The person's name was "Red."

"I bet he played the piano or guitar," Rob said in amazement.

"Or maybe he was a famous singer," Brittnye suggested.

"Whatever he was, I'll bet he was fun," Rob said as he outlined the notes with his fingers. "I think I want a space shuttle carved on my tombstone. You can all remember me as the 'mad scientist.'"

"Very funny, Robbie," Brittnye said. "Then, I'll have a little cat on mine because I love my kitten."

"Hey, Dad can have a golf club on his." Rob fell to the grassy hillside and began laughing. "And Mom can have a computer on hers."

By this time our entire family was laughing and teasing each other about special idiosyncrasies, hobbies, and interests.

" . . . and Ashley can have a piano carved on hers, and Aunt Lori can have . . ." Brittnye's voice trailed behind her as she skipped over the red clay on the backside of the hill.

I sat for a moment alone under the large tree and looked over the numerous tombstones. These people were all alive once. To some families, the memories of these people are still alive. As I absorbed the view, I was aware of the cross on the steeple of the red brick church across the street and high on the hill; it seemed to frame the old cemetery. "Beneath the cross of Jesus," I hummed softly as I stood and started back to the street below.

Accepting death as a part of life is healthy. But sharing its burden of sorrow along with the hope of eternal life in Jesus Christ is vital teaching for our children. For facing death needs to be shared in the context of our Christian faith and the promises it holds.

Visiting a cemetery is just one way to encourage children to begin thinking about their own mortality and eternal salvation. We found it to be an experience that led very naturally into lessons on life as our young children developed a solid foundation in their Christian faith.

Suggestions for Talking About Death With Children

1. Realize that there are no easy answers. So it is especially important for the parent to create an atmosphere of love and reassurance as the family discusses this subject.

2. Each child interprets and responds to the subject of death differently, depending on his experiences, knowledge, and maturity level. Allow for this uniqueness as you share feelings, knowledge, and ideas.

3. Give your child straightforward answers. Don't cover up when death occurs. Closed doors, whispering, and sending the child off to a neighbor's house when there is a death in your family only adds to their fear of the unknown.

4. Talk about a pet or a plant that has died. This will enable the child to begin to open up about his worries and feelings about death.

5. Share with your child memories of loved ones who have died. This enables your child to reaffirm that people continue to be in our memories.

6. Emphasize the teachings of Jesus Christ as found in the Scriptures. Eternal life is promised for all believers and is the hope of our Christian faith. If you have questions regarding

eternal life, make an appointment with your pastor to sort through your beliefs. If you are confident in what you believe, you will radiate that belief and assurance to your children.

17

Not to Worry

"Cast all your anxiety on him because he cares for you."
—1 Peter 5:7

"I just know that party at the beach won't be chaperoned," I said to my husband over the phone that rainy Friday morning. "I'm not certain, but Rob sounded hesitant when I asked him to tell me which parents would be there. Do you think he's hiding something?"

"Now, quit worrying," Bob said trying to calm me down. "You are going to have to trust him. After all, he's seventeen and has never disappointed you yet."

That's just the problem, I thought to myself as I hung up the phone. *At some point he just has to disappoint us. I mean I've read too much about teenage parties, and I've been a teen. I know what can happen when teenagers are together late at night without a responsible adult. And I know how impulsive kids can be.*

"Quit worrying," my husband had recommended. Quit worrying? I worried all day. I worried about what could happen as our son drove home from the beach late at night. I fretted about what other teenagers might entice him to do. I toyed with thoughts of alcohol, too much freedom, teenage pranks, wet streets, and flat tires. I worried while I washed dishes, while I rode my exercise bicycle, and while I ironed the family's clothes. I worried secretly while my friend told me about her upcoming cruise. I even worried about the approaching beach party while

I had my daily devotions. I still worried even while I gave all my problems to God. I worried until my son came home from school at 3:30.

"Hi Mom," our young son said as he dropped his books on the table. He walked back to his room to open his mail then added, "Oh, by the way, we decided not to go to Greg's party at the beach tonight. We heard that some guys from another school were coming to start trouble, and they were bringing beer. Greg even admitted that his parents might not be there so we're all going to a movie instead. I don't trust Greg sometimes. Is that all right?"

All right? All right!—after I had spent an entire day worrying about what could happen to my firstborn son?

Once I was over the shock from the change in plans, I admitted my embarrassment to myself. I laughed aloud to relieve my inner tension, then called my husband and said softly so Rob couldn't hear, "Guess what? He's not going to the party . . . He decided that it wasn't his style so he and Nancy are going to a movie instead."

"And how was your day, dear?" my husband asked knowingly and seemed to even chuckle. "Did you fret and stew and worry all day?"

"Me? Oh, maybe for just a few minutes," I tried to sound in control, then gave in. "Yes, I thought about everything that could happen the entire day until he came home. It actually ruined my day."

"It" didn't actually ruin my day, I thought later. I had allowed my mind to dwell on it and that ruined my day. The worry habit didn't stop there.

Several weekends later was the junior-senior prom. All the teens were going, and they were going to stay out until the wee hours of the morning. All the teens were going to attend parties around the city, and all the teens were going to go to breakfast at 4:00 A.M. All the teens? That's what my teenager said. That's what started my worries again.

What if all the teens go to a party that is unchaperoned? What if all the teens bring alcohol to these parties? What if all the teens start racing around town in their cars and get into an accident? What if there is a fight with teens from another school? What if someone gets hurt? What if they can't reach us because our telephone is off the hook or out of order? If it could be worried about, I did it.

"We will come home around midnight to change clothes, then we are going to go to Rick's party, then to breakfast. We'll be home by 3:00 A.M." my son reassured me as he and his date came by for pictures. "Mom, don't worry. I'm in control, and I'll be careful."

I watched him leave in his black tuxedo, looking so mature and in control. But was he really?

Everything was fine until midnight. Bob and I were trying to sleep when Rob came into the room.

"Mom, I'm home. We are changing into shorts and T-shirts, then we're going to drive to another party over at the beach," he said softly. "Yes, there are chaperones. I will be very careful and I promise to be home by 3:00 A.M."

The beach? A party at the beach? Agggh! My worries started again.

"Oh, Rob. What about Rick's party?" I pleaded softly. "It's down the street. Why don't you go there instead? There are so many accidents on prom night."

"We just came from Rick's party, and everyone is going to the beach for a while. Don't worry Mom, I'll be very careful."

I lay still for a minute as the seventeen-year-old walked quietly out of our room. I knew he would be careful. But would the other drivers on the street be just as careful?

I tossed and turned for three hours. Even though my son's words, *"Don't worry, Mom,"* went through my head, I still heard ambulances racing down the highway and imagined that the phone rang several times. I jumped up startled as I heard noises outside, noises inside, and noises that weren't even noises. I counted the seconds on the clock and even took my pulse a few times while I waited for my son to return home. *Come on 3:00 A.M. Hurry up so our son will come home.*

At 2:55 A.M. my mind was reeling with imaginary situations that my son could have gotten into while he was on the highway on prom night. *I'll get out of bed,* I thought. *I'll go get some milk and wait for him to come in.*

I tiptoed down the long hallway to the other end of the house and closed the doors behind me. When I opened the door to the den I heard the television on. I stumbled in the dark to go turn the set off and saw my son sleeping on the couch.

"Rob, Rob." I called his name as I shook him. "What in the world are you doing?"

"Uh? Oh, Mom," he said sleepily. "Nancy and I decided not to go to the party at the beach after all. We stayed here and watched a video instead. We both were so tired that I took her home an hour ago and came back and fell asleep on the couch."

"You mean you have been here the entire time?" I asked in disbelief. "You didn't go to the party at the beach?"

"Oh, that? No, Nancy didn't want to go. She was pretty tired from cheerleading practice so we changed our plans. I closed all the doors so we wouldn't disturb you and Dad. Sure hope we didn't wake you up."

Wake me up? Did I ever go to sleep that night? Did my imagination ever stop to let me sleep peacefully?

"Oh, don't worry Rob," I answered truthfully. "You were so quiet we honestly didn't know you were here."

If only we had known. I walked back to my room and punished myself over and over for the worries I created, worries that were completely unfounded since my son was home the entire time.

The next morning I sat at the breakfast table and tried to read the paper with red, bloodshot eyes from lack of sleep.

"What's the matter, Deb?" my husband asked as he got ready to go to the church to study for his sermon. "You look like you didn't sleep at all last night?"

Sleep? Are parents of teenagers supposed to sleep when all they do is worry, fret, and dwell on their children's activities?

"Bob, do you know that Rob was here in the den watching a video last night while we thought he was at that beach party?" I wanted Bob to be as surprised as I was of the change of plans.

"Rob always makes good choices, doesn't he?" Bob said smiling.

"Yeah, I know. We've raised him right," I said smugly. "You're right. He hasn't disappointed us yet. I guess it is time. . . . "

"Time for what?" Bob interrupted, smiling.

"Time to let go and trust him," I answered hesitantly. And to myself I thought, *Yes, it's time to quit worrying and let our firstborn son grow up.*

"He took my hand tenderly and whispered, 'You are my best friend! I'd rather be with you than anyone else.'"

 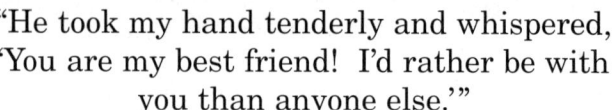

18

"My Wife, My Best Friend"

"Greater love has no one than this, that he lay down his life for his friends."

—John 15:13

"This is my wife, my best friend," my husband proudly announced as he introduced me to the other couples at an alumni banquet several years ago. I was surprised; other husbands had used such romantic terms as "my beautiful better half" and "the love of my life." When I heard the words "best friend," at first I had visions of Bob's feeling I was his buddy, one of the guys. But as we sat down at the table after the introductions, I decided that I had been paid the highest compliment a spouse could receive. He took my hand tenderly and whispered, "You are my best friend! I'd rather be with you than anyone else."

As I reflected on the term "best friend" later that evening, I had to chuckle. How meaningful it is when two people can be married, stay in love, and yet keep alive that special liking for each other that enables them to grow as best friends!

One dictionary describes a friend as "a person whom one knows well; an intimate acquaintance; a person on the same side of the struggle." To be this "person whom one knows well" to your spouse, you must continue to give time, energy, and nurture to the relationship. Such care seeks only good for the other—the same self-giving love Jesus taught in the Gospels:

"Greater love has no one than this, that he lay down his life for his friends" (John 15:13).

What does it mean to lay down your life for your spouse? It involves getting to know not only the partner's ups and downs, but fears, goals, and dreams. And once you know your spouse's needs, you work at fulfilling them. Placing someone else's needs in front of your own isn't easy. But recall that when your children were very young, you probably did a lot of such self-giving. Of course, when it's another adult who has the needs, our response is not quite so automatic. And if you give without getting in return, as the marriage continues, making a positive response grows tougher. Stumbling blocks such as resentment, selfishness, anxieties, and fears surface and can be destructive to the marriage relationship.

The Bible speaks often of friendships. "A friend loves at all times, and a brother is born for adversity" (Proverbs 17:17). "Each of you should look not only to your own interests, but also to the interests of others" (Philippians 2:4). Other Scripture passages speak of "bearing one another's burdens" and "loving as Christ loved the church."

But even with the encouragement we get from the Scriptures to have friends, such relationships must be constantly nourished.

Strengthening and nurturing that much-needed friendship requires constant marriage "maintenance" by both partners. It begins by first accepting oneself. To like another person, we must first look inward and accept what we see. This does not mean we have to like everything about ourselves, for each of us has traits and habits that could be improved. Nevertheless, acceptance of oneself is the key to establishing friendship in a marriage.

Some older friends in our congregation have been married for over forty years. They speak of working at being together regularly to listen, to understand, and to be understood. According to them, "A special night together is a delicious meal and time for lingering conversation. This can spark any relationship. Or adopting one certain night for 'date night' can add sparkle to a mundane relationship—even if it's just a walk through the neighborhood."

And just because the marriage has lasted for many years does not mean that it can't use the spark of fun and enthusiasm.

Some couples benefit by participating in the same recreational activities—golfing, bowling, tennis—building their friendship while playing together. Other couples find working together in the same career a way to realize their goals and maintain togetherness. As a hobby, some friends of ours began to write fiction for young adults, which they did together in the evenings. In the course of enjoying the writing, they began to learn more of each other's inner feelings, emotions, and dreams.

My husband and I are fortunate enough to enjoy working in a local church together. We organize activities for the young people, teach in various workshops, and lead family-centered seminars. This allows us to share the message of Christ, and we also learn more about each other. As we lead discussions, our own feelings, values, and goals are revealed to each other. To get involved together in a project, hobby, or sport may seem like too much work for some couples, but to others it is recognized as marriage maintenance.

Couples who seek to become best friends must make time to share their feelings, goals, hurts, and joys. Marriage enrichment seminars encourage couples to write letters to each other, expressing those same intimate feelings, especially if communication is lacking. A counselor friend who leads weekend marriage enrichment classes said, "Exposing yourself to someone else is risky. You may say too much, resulting in hurt feelings. At other times, the other person may not communicate at all, bringing more hurt feelings. For growth to take place, communication must occur regularly. As communication continues, you learn how much to say, and when and how to say it. To be honest, yet not to intentionally inflict pain on the other person, requires tact. To be tactful requires knowing the other person so well that you know what will injure and what will nurture."

I have learned that tact involves not criticizing my husband's sermons until at least the following Tuesday, and then only if I bring out some positive points first. He has found that any criticism of my cooking, especially a dish that required much time and preparation, should be made a few days after it has been eaten.

Becoming best friends in a marriage involves sacrifice. For some couples it may mean a night at the ballet to please one spouse and sitting on the hard bleachers at a football game in freezing temperatures to please the other. In our marriage this sacrifice involves my watching Sunday afternoon sports, without too much grumbling, and my husband periodically escorts me window-shopping.

Staying best friends in a marriage also requires some individual solitude—time with God in study and prayer; time to plan the day or week; and time to read, think, and meditate.

On our honeymoon I felt demeaned and hurt when my husband of seven days told me he needed to be alone and retreated to the extra bedroom to read. I laugh about this incident now, for I have come to realize the importance of time alone. Quiet time should be worked into the family routine because spiritual inspiration—a time to listen to God and become aware of spiritual needs—is essential to growth, both personal and marital.

Growing as best friends requires that each marriage partner remain independent enough to realize and cultivate his or her own talents and unique gifts. Generally most people marry because of physical attraction combined with compatibility and common interests. As the marriage develops and matures, differences are uncovered. These differences can strengthen the partnership. Special traits and unique gifts can be the spice in a marriage. When one partner becomes too dependent on another, loneliness and despair can result—especially if the stronger partner is injured or disabled.

Maintaining a relationship that encourages liking and respecting each other as friends demands that the workload be shared. Lori, a working mother of two preschoolers, said, "Neither of us enjoys housework but we know it has to be done. We usually divide the chores, with each of us picking the most and least favorite."

Being best friends in marriage doesn't mean problems never arise. In fact, if the marriage is argument free, then someone is probably being stepped on! But problems in a marriage can halt growth only if both persons resist compromise; on the other hand, problems can produce growth if the couple is determined to make the relationship work. If problems are tackled in a positive, productive manner, the marriage can be enhanced.

How's your busy schedule? In the midst of raising children do you allow times for nurturing your marriage relationship? The following suggestions for doing so even when there is little time may be helpful.

1. Take a little time each day to be alone with your spouse. Touch base, for example, each evening, or make a point to meet for lunch during a busy week. Talk about your spouse's interests—and listen! Is your spouse lonely? or neglected? Is your spouse hurting due to personal conflict or inner turmoil? Try to read between the lines as you converse and relate a message of caring. Paul teaches us to think not just about our own affairs, but to be interested in others and in what they are doing. A real friend makes time in a busy schedule to care for others.

2. Communicate friendship with your spouse through physical touch. A pat on the shoulder, a warm hug, a squeeze of the hand, can express caring and concern without sexual implications. In a marriage that includes friendship, a warm touch may be the extra reassurance your spouse needs during the day.

3. Share your joys and concerns with your spouse. Friendships can often become one-sided. Therefore, you must also communicate your personal joys and concerns to your spouse. Share your faith in God, your ups and downs, your goals and fears. Let your spouse know of the struggles in your life. As you take time to build an honest friendship in your marriage, your spouse can become even more sensitive to your inner needs. Paul teaches in Galatians 6:2, "Carry each other's burdens, and in this way you will fulfill the law of Christ." Personal sharing is vital to a genuine, long-lasting friendship in marriage.

4. Stand up for your spouse. "A friend loves at all times, and a brother is born for adversity" (Proverbs 17:17). When you are your spouse's best friend, you believe in this person no matter what happens. This often means supporting your spouse when personal trials overwhelm him, telling other family members of the good qualities of your spouse.

Some marriage partners only pretend to be friends. A true friend is loyal and takes risks in supporting the other. A true friend in a marriage doesn't hesitate to stick up for the other.

5. Forgive your spouse. We all make mistakes; no one is innocent of this. A true friend is able to forgive the other and move on into a closer relationship. A true friend in a marriage is also able to accept the forgiveness of the other, which is often the most difficult to do. Remember, forgiveness is the essence of the Gospels. This forgiveness should be a part of our caring relationship with our spouse.

Through communication, regular times together alone, sacrifice, solitude, and continuous giving, most marital relationships can grow into best friendships, becoming a strong foundation for the marriage and an example for the children to follow. Like anything else worth having, becoming best friends in marriage takes time, effort, and caring.

19
Speaking with Sensitivity

"We are meant to speak the truth in love, and to grow up in every way into Christ."

—Ephesians 4:15, Phillips

My friend Linda's second-grade daughter is known for being honest. Last Wednesday when she told her math teacher that his shirt was wrinkled and much too old to wear to school, Linda was called to school.

"I don't understand," my frustrated friend said in despair after a lecture from the school's principal. "Nicki has always been encouraged to tell the truth. Can we train her to hold back some unkind truths?"

In our own family we are sometimes confronted with children who think they know all of life's answers. Several years ago, that's how our oldest son answered a visiting theology professor's question.

"And what will you be when you grow up?" the wise professor asked our son at a formal dinner party. "Will you follow in your father's footsteps and be a pastor?"

"Actually, Reverend Burns," Rob spoke with great boyish confidence, "I don't think so. The hours of a minister are much too long and the pay scale is pretty low for today's standards."

Another painful memory of truth-telling is of the time our middle daughter blurted out loudly at a church dinner,

"Whoever cooked this squash casserole sure can't cook!" I cringed and my face flushed as all eyes looked at me.

Of course, as parents we have learned to let such childish remarks glance off our toughened skin. We discuss the matter later—behind closed doors. But what about training our children to be honest with their communication without being abusive? Is this a possibility?

Being honest can be perplexing to a child. If he is too honest, like young Nicki was, people will accuse him of being rude and inconsiderate. Then when the child hides his real feelings and tells people what they want to hear, people may think he is insincere. Can your child ever give his honest opinion?

Telling the truth and being honest is an admirable quality. But how something is said can be just as important. Facial expressions and other body language, or the tone and inflection of voice, can communicate even more powerfully than words.

At least as significant as being honest in our communication is the reason for that honesty—the motive behind the message. Some people can be cruel with their honesty. It's one thing for a three-year-old to point to a man in the checkout line and exclaim: "That man has a big tummy." It's quite another for a Christian to tell someone, "You look dowdy in those new glasses." The three-year-old is simply identifying and confirming the concept "big." Some adults, on the other hand, realize that their words can hurt but say them anyway.

When people are secure and happy with themselves, they have no need to put others down. On the contrary, a sign of security and maturity is the ability to develop a relationship of mutual support in which there is positive criticism. Honesty is an important element in mature relationships. Nevertheless, how and why truthful words are spoken is just as important.

How honest is your child? Does he constantly confront others with the whole truth, as painful as it may be, or has he learned to temper his honest communication with tact?

Tact is that delicate perception of knowing the right thing to say or do without offending the other person. When you use tact in talking with others without distorting the truth in any way, growth can occur. You use tact in relationships because you care about the other person and how he or she feels. This involves speaking the truth with the right motive and with the hope of serving the friendship rather than undermining it.

Think back. Remember the 60s slogan "Tell it like it is"? Youth directed it at the establishment, but soon aimed it at whomever. If someone was overweight, you told him. If you didn't like a friend's hair, you said so. But being indiscriminately open and honest hurts people and damages their self-esteem. No apparent growth results from such blunt communication. Honesty is one goal for Christians, but it should be balanced with kindness and compassion.

Many times we may be claiming to speak truth (that is, fact) when it is merely opinion, judgment—and that based on insufficient evidence. Childish statements such as "My brother is a brat" and "Her dress is really gross" are opinions, not facts.

You can help your child learn the difference by using the following examples. Ask your child to determine which is fact and which is opinion:

- Sandy's bicycle is ugly. (opinion)
- Sandy's bicycle is seven years old. (fact)
- Randy's shoes are torn at the toe. (fact)
- Randy's shoes are for geeks. (opinion)
- Mr. Martin is a very mean man. (opinion)
- Mr. Martin makes his children go to bed very early. (fact)

The Bible offers guidance for speaking the truth with tact. Share the following Scripture passages with your child as guidelines for Christian communication.

- Ephesians 4:15: "Speak the truth in love" (Phillips).
- Ephesians 4:25: "Put off falsehood and speak truthfully."
- Philippians 4:8: "Finally, brothers, whatever is true, whatever is noble, whatever is right, whatever is pure, whatever is lovely, whatever is admirable, if anything is excellent or praiseworthy—think about such things."

In the Gospels Jesus teaches us a life-style of empathy, of being sensitive to those around us. This selfless love that He gives enables us to meet the personal needs of our family and friends, rather than tearing them down.

Helping our children develop into honest, mature Christian

adults is the primary goal of parenting. Still, they must make their own judgments about what is truth and what is mere opinion. Children need to learn how to measure truth and decide if what they say is going to hurt others.

Asking the following questions can help your children learn to consider their judgments before they speak. These questions can help determine that fine line between truth and opinion. Teach these insights to your children. You might want to join them in acting out how to respond in each situation.

1. *Have I ever been faced with this situation in my own life?*

Your child can often temper truthful statements by acknowledging personal faults or shortcomings. This vulnerability about one's self helps to create an atmosphere of warmth and acceptance for the other person. If your child can show support in the situation they're discussing, the chances are great that no abrupt judgments will be offered.

2. *How would I like to hear the message?*

Compassion, sincerity, and empathy communicate your feelings of friendship and support. To have empathy means to be sensitive to the needs of others. A child who has empathy will look for the best in his friend. A relationship that really works and involves personal caring means going that extra mile—together! Messages given in this setting are more likely to be taken kindly and, perhaps, open the eyes of the friend to a better way.

3. *Do I really hear what my friend is saying?*

The world is crying out for love and affirmation. Listening skills are essential to making people feel loved and affirmed, as well as for letting them feel understood. If your child comes across as unyielding when he communicates honestly with his friend, the friend may simply close up, feeling that talking about the situation has become useless. Teach your child to try to relate to what the other person is saying without judging, then he will open the door to continued communication in the relationship.

4. *Will the statement help our friendship grow?*

Positive truths spoken in love can enhance friendships. When your child thoughtlessly shares critical opinions, he only destroys the communication between himself and the other person. Children must learn this, often by trial and error, so they might develop close, meaningful relationships.

5. *What will my friend's reaction be?*

Teach your child to think before he speaks, considering how the other person will react to what he is going to say. Is the friend overly sensitive or insecure? Perhaps the statement could be misinterpreted and give offense. A good rule of thumb is to count to ten before making a statement that could be considered critical. This allows the speaker time to gain control, sort out his thoughts, consider the effect of his words, and think about alternatives before speaking.

6. *What is my reason for speaking the truth?*

Many people speak certain truths merely to build themselves up; for example, Lynne told her best friend Mary, "I like you a lot, but you are so sloppy and fat."

Lynne's statement was obviously her personal opinion. Share this with your child and ask, "Did Lynne offer the criticism to help Mary or to make herself seem better?"

7. *Can I express my personal taste in a positive manner?*

Your child can state opinions tactfully if he says them sensitively.

- "Your new bicycle is terrific! I prefer ten-speeds myself."
- "The way you layer your clothes looks great on you. I prefer to wear my shirt tucked in."
- "The new sweatshirt is really neat. I like to wear nylon jackets in cold weather."

Using affirmation or a positive statement along with the personal opinion makes the opinion sound more like simply an expression of personal preference rather than an expression of superior taste.

8. *Will the statement still be true a week from now?*

"You make me so mad! I will never speak to you again." Sometimes a crusade of telling all one thinks can ruin friendships. Time is a key factor in healing wounds and changing situations between people. Teach your child to think about tomorrow, next week if possible, before he attempts to tell friends exactly how he feels.

Being honest and open is important in your child's concept of being Christian. Equally important to speaking the truth is that your child learn to speak the truth in a tactful, positive manner, striving to comfort, affirm, and build up the other person.

20

Respected Children Respect

"Show proper respect to everyone."

—1 Peter 2:17

I chuckled as I leafed through an old family album recently. My grandmother was in a picture as a young teen. Instead of showing a fun-loving smile, she was perched atop a hard, wooden stool, her head held uncomfortably high and her lips pressed tight—hardly the image of a normal fifteen-year-old.

"Ah, yes," Granny said later as I showed her the picture. "I remember those days. That portrait is over seventy years old. We dared not smile in the picture for fear Papa would punish us. My, how times have changed!"

Remember the days of yesteryear? Children were to be seen and not heard. Schools used the method of education described in the children's rhyme, "Reading, 'riting, and 'rithmetic; taught by the rule of the hickory stick." If my grandmother is any indication, children of her generation obeyed those strict rules and did not challenge authority.

What has happened? Has there been a loss of respect for parental authority, and is it our fault or theirs?

I watched a thirteen-year-old boy belittle his father during church last Sunday. "I don't have to listen to you," the handsome boy said in a loud whisper as others watched.

His disrespectful remark did not concern me as much as the

way his parent dealt with it. Embarrassed, the father tried to ignore the comment. He finally let the teen do what he wanted—skip the worship service. No confrontation. No negotiation. The child simply did as he pleased.

That incident left a vivid imprint on my mind. Can you teach your children to respect authority? Is there a secret for winning this respect?

The Bible teaches us to "Train a child in the way he should go, and when he is old he will not turn from it" (Proverbs 22:6). But this suggests authority, and unfortunately the word "authority" often has negative connotations for some parents. A friend of mine told me she cannot stand to say no to her only child, a two-year-old. She said, "I am here to love our child, not to be involved in power struggles." I wanted to tell her that a parent shows real love by taking a firm stand on everyday issues, that love and discipline go together.

Set limits for your child, allowing activities that are age-appropriate. Discuss these limits periodically. Follow through with a proper reprimand or consequence if a limit is intentionally broken. This allows you to fulfill your duty as an authority in the home.

Part of this inability to say no stems from our fear of offending others. We also hesitate to say no because we don't want to be thought of as harsh. However, if we think about it, we must conclude that yes is not always the caring answer to our children, not if we know the consequences will be negative, that they will be hurt in the long run. It takes courage and strength, but we must say no if we feel our child is in some way at risk by an activity or added commitment.

Empathy, not sympathy, is important as you are sensitive to your child's needs. Empathy is trying to put yourself in your child's shoes so you know how he feels. A parent-child relationship that really works and has respect means going that extra mile—together.

Having empathy for your child includes seeking the best for him. A friend said, "When Jason asked to go away last summer to be a counselor at a resort, I immediately said no. After thinking about it for a few days, I realized Jason needed time away from us. He was old enough and mature enough to handle this experience, and I wanted him to know what it is like to be on his own."

Having empathy might also be described as showing the love Jesus taught. This love seeks the best for the other person; it is a selfless love. "Love means never having to say you're sorry" is pure fiction. Real love frequently says I'm sorry. Apologies when needed, along with God's forgiveness, are necessary for building deep relationships. When you admit being wrong, you say to your child "I respect you and your feelings."

The I-don't-care attitude can destroy respect in a Christian home. The parent, especially, should have an I-care attitude, especially when no one else does. As you are making decisions, reaching out with God's love, and being genuine and open, you are exposing your children to a picture of respect that will eventually develop in their own lives.

As you train your children to respect you, think of yourself as a stationary planet with many satellites revolving around you. For your child, you are the best Christian he knows. Every word you say, every action you take, is interpreted by your child as guidelines for living.

While it is important for children to respect adults, it is also important that adults treat children with respect. Children learn to respect other adults as they are shown respect by their parents. A friend with two adopted children said, "I have found it helpful to ask myself, 'Would I say that to a friend?' before speaking. Also, when I discipline my children, I always try to make sure the discipline fits the misdeed. Most of our small discipline problems are eliminated by talking through negative situations and letting the children help to establish family rules."

Share your life with your child. Talk with him about faith and how God moves in your life. Listen to his prayer concerns and keep these in mind as you pray each day.

Most important, you can't share a Christlike love and respect with your child if you aren't being spiritually fed. The caring parent must make time to become filled with knowledge, insight, and the wisdom of the Scriptures. This involves regular worship at church, participation in a class or small group, and personal Bible study and prayer. As your child sees you showing respect for God and your church, he will have a role model to follow.

The Bible is full of terms such as "honor," "obey," and "respect," which we must continue to teach our children. As we relay these messages through our attitudes, words, and actions toward them, we are conveying these attributes to our children.

Parenting isn't easy in the nineties. But with a little concern and a lot of thought and prayer, a Christian parent can lead the way by living out respect in the home.

21
Handling Blue Days

"Why are you downcast, O my soul? Why so disturbed within me? Put your hope in God."

—Psalm 42:5

Rob gazed out his bedroom window at the new day. The weather was perfect for the football game his friends had planned the night before. The sky was a bright blue. The warm sun was melting the remaining frost off the brown grass. Rob could see Chris and Jason walking down the street to the empty lot as he was getting ready for the big game. Yet something was wrong. Somehow, my son felt as if he carried a tremendous load on his shoulders. He felt lonely and small in his secure world.

Does your child experience times like that? Some parents might call it the blahs, or simply feeling down. As the child starts his day, he feels weighted down with the problems of his world, complaining that "everyone and everything is against me." On these "blue days" nothing seems to go the way it should.

Take heart. Everyone experiences this emptiness or loneliness. As adults, most of us know we can feel lost even in a crowd or with our best friends. In fact, this dull, empty feeling can occur with or without company. Why we sometimes wake up feeling this way is a mystery. On the other hand, the feeling can be intensified when we begin to dwell on ourselves. The blues set in usually when we center our thoughts on our fear and rejection. The more we remain aware of these negative feelings and ignore the needs of those around us, the more lonely and empty we become.

Of course, loneliness and being alone are two different things. We know from the Scriptures that being alone, as illustrated by the life of Jesus, need not be a time for feeling sorry for oneself. In fact, Scripture passages indicate that when Christ was in solitude, He found His source of power. Matthew 14:23 says that after spending the day preaching and teaching the great crowds, "He went up on a mountainside by himself to pray." Luke implies that it was a pattern: "Jesus often withdrew to lonely places and prayed" (Luke 5:16).

"Singing the blues," "having the blahs," doesn't mean your child must focus on feelings of depression and loneliness. Instead, encourage your child to use these moments as a vital part of the day to organize his activities, set personal goals, and be at one with God in prayer, Bible study, and meditation. As your child begins to tune out his surroundings, he is more apt to hear that "gentle whisper" of our Lord.

Perhaps the following suggestions will help your child cope when he feels lonely or depressed.

Become Inspired

Encourage your child to use his off-days to become inspired. As he does so, he may find new discoveries about his inner-self. Let's look at some ways of doing this.

1. Keep a journal—writing down feelings at the moment (if the Lord brought you through it once, He can do it again).

2. Keep prayer lists—praying for friends and family members.

3. Set daily goals and weekly goals—post these goals on a bulletin board in the bedroom as a reminder.

4. Read inspirational books—find books on how others have handled adversity.

5. Read the Scriptures and quote key verses—find strength in Bible verses that relate to life situations.

6. Write poems, haiku—try to identify personal feelings in creative verse. Keep a notebook nearby for this.

7. Write letters—use this time to write to old friends or relatives.

8. Write songs—music can lift the soul! Try writing new lyrics to popular tunes.

Listen to God

Encourage your child to allow God to speak in his life. We often spend so much time pleading with God for our way that we may not listen for His answer.

Your child can write down thoughts and messages that he feels are of God. While doing so, he can also become aware of God's presence through personal prayer and study of the Scriptures. God can also speak through others—parents, teachers, ministers, close friends. The child must learn to allow God to speak to him and then to really listen when God speaks.

As your child uses times of loneliness to listen to God, his relationship with the Lord will deepen.

Live One Day at a Time

Remind your child that yesterday is past; tomorrow is not yet here—but today is his for living! Jesus affirms this when He said in Matthew 6:34: "Therefore do not worry about tomorrow, for tomorrow will worry about itself. Each day has enough trouble of its own."

Many of us dwell on our mistakes. "If only I had studied harder for that biology test, maybe I could have pulled a B." Or, "If only I had asked permission to take the car to the store, I might not have bumped into the neighbor's mailbox."

Encourage your child to let go of the past and take each day as it comes, enjoying the good times of the moment. The reality of the Christian faith is for the present. We cannot change yesterday; worrying about the past by saying "if only" simply produces anxiety and never solves the problem.

Two Heads Are Better Than One

When your child does feel blue, try to get him to share his feelings with you or a close friend. Even if he can't identify the initial cause of the depression, talking about himself may still bring helpful insight. Or engaging in conversation with someone else may help take his mind off the problem long enough for him to see a positive side.

Groups, such as church youth programs, a club at school, or an athletic team are excellent sources for finding support and a sense of belonging. Your child can share his problems and others can empathize with him, for they have likely experienced similar feelings.

Exercise and Proper Diet Help, Too!

Brisk walks after dinner, balanced meals during the week, and fresh air do wonders for such feelings (nowadays we are told by the medical community that it has to do with our body's production of something called endorphins). Your child will feel healthier and his problems will seem less as he begins to handle life's stresses more effectively.

Other hints for helping your child handle blue days include the following:

1. Keep a positive attitude. For example, encourage your child to visualize a funny situation when depressing thoughts creep into his mind. As he begins to learn to replace depressing thoughts with uplifting thoughts, he is gaining a skill in handling blue days.

2. Realize that feeling down is temporary. Coping with a blue day is easier if your child realizes that the simple passage of time can sometimes cure us. Remind him that usually tomorrow will be brighter.

3. Pace activities. Often the low your child feels is the result of putting out an unusual amount of energy—after a midterm exam, a big game, or a major holiday party. By slowing down during the busy times and saving some energy for the next week, the low won't hit quite so hard.

Concern, not worry, is the key to your child's coping with feelings of loneliness and depression. Worry saps our strength, but concern allows us to remain objective in our thinking.

Does your child have a positive, productive life, and still feels blue from time to time? Remember, overcoming temporary low points must come from within. As your child begins to open up and share his feelings with someone else, lives one day at a time, and regularly spends time with the Heavenly Father, the blues will be handled more easily.

22
Avoiding Manipulation

"How good and pleasant it is when brothers live together in unity!"

—Psalm 133:1

My daughter Brittnye looked up at me with her soft, brown eyes and spoke. "Please, Mom. If you let me stay up and watch this television show, I promise I will clean both bathrooms in the morning."

Her older brother, Rob, chimed in, using all of his persuasive skills: "And I'll watch Ashley while you write, and even take her on a bike ride after breakfast tomorrow."

I thought for a moment, weighed the alternatives, and weakly gave in to their desires to stay up later. Somehow, at that moment, having the bathrooms cleaned and free time to write seemed more appealing than following the bedtime rules of the home.

Have you ever been manipulated by your child? Defined as concealed control, manipulation can occur as your child communicates a message to you, and you unknowingly are persuaded to think, act, or do as he or she wants. Manipulation can also occur when your child ignores your question or advice. And you can also manipulate your child as you seek to always get your way.

Manipulation in our families involves placing our own demands and expectations on those around us. We tend to make the child or other family member feel unloved or guilty. Then once the child gives in to our way of thinking, we reward him generously.

Manipulation is not good for a healthy parent-child relationship. The person who is the manipulator often resorts to using blackmail to get his way. The manipulator tends to make deals with the other person, such as "I will let you go to the party if you will stay home and help clean the house today." Or the child could be the aggressor saying, "If I get straight A's will you let me get a new bike?"

The person who is being manipulated experiences feelings of helplessness, anger, and frustration. This person often gives in for fear of losing the love of the other person in the relationship.

As we manipulate our children and are manipulated by them, we lose a part of our identity. Standards we believe in become weak as we give in to the child's persuasion. Values are compromised as the child (or parent) bribes the other person into thinking his way or doing as he wants. Persons who are manipulated often become people who do not know what they believe, cannot distinguish right from wrong, and are continually used by those around them.

Can we avoid being manipulated and used by our children? How can we as Christian parents stop manipulating our children and develop a more genuine, lasting relationship?

Before we can begin to show fairness and consideration to others, we must first begin to accept who we are. This includes our shortcomings as well as our assets. Once a decision is made to accept ourselves and develop those positive points we have, we can then begin to accept those around us. Realizing that everyone is different is a vital step in accepting others.

Joan, a middle-aged woman and parent of a seventeen-year-old son, was experiencing dramatic role changes. As her son began to make plans to enter college, she felt lost and alone. Her world had involved just her child for many years. When she felt threatened by her son, Joan would withhold her affection or ignore him. Then on her first job, no one seemed to care whether Joan was angry or hurting inside.

"Once I began to identify my own talents, strengths, and weaknesses, I was really able to accept who I am. My image of being 'coy, demure, in-control Joan' was no longer acceptable or real. I believe my new self is much more likeable and genuine. Now I can see others, especially my son, in a more caring way." Joan shared these insights at a spiritual growth retreat at our church.

To avoid manipulating others, we must realize that we are not always right. Many parents do not listen to their child's ideas; although they may feel their ideas are the best ones, this attitude can lead into a habit of always seeking control, which is a form of manipulation. When parents limit their resources to just their own ideas and opinions, growth is stifled.

On the other hand, in creative problem solving, groups of people are able to zero in on the best solution or idea through brainstorming sessions. Identifying the problem, sharing creative solutions, then agreeing on the best course of action is done without anyone in the group being manipulated.

In solving problems fairly in our family relationships, we can also use this method. A family council, or meeting, is a perfect way for the sharing of ideas on a regular basis. Ask for ideas, innovative solutions, facts, and past experiences. Weigh the pros and cons together with your child. Identify the consequences and the alternatives in the situation. Then arrive at an agreeable solution. Compromise is an important concept in developing an honest, fair relationship. Agreement occurs as parent and child experience give-and-take, as ideas are openly expressed and opinions shared, and as family members accept one another on equal terms.

Parents need to express themselves honestly. Sarah, a fourth grader, wanted a stereo like her best friend's. Her parents felt this was not the proper time for Sarah to have a stereo, so they refused. After a heated debate one evening, Sarah's father finally shared his personal feelings with his daughter.

"Sarah," he said gently, "even if we did have the money to purchase an elaborate stereo system for you, I would not. The idea is too extravagant for a ten-year-old. If you received a stereo now, what would you look forward to as a teen?"

By sharing his personal feelings, risking rejection by his child, Sarah's father ended the debate. And Sarah was able to grow as her father verbalized his opinion and helped her understand why the answer was no.

Children can be quite eloquent and very convincing. To avoid being manipulated by your child, you must first decide what you think or feel about a subject or issue. Then you need to work at verbalizing it. Trust yourself to make wise decisions, based on the fact that you truly love your child and want what is best for him. Pray about this matter and trust God to lead you in guiding your child.

Donna, a mother of a bright fifth grader, overheard a conversation he was having with his peers. "I was shocked when I realized how much he knew about the world we live in," Donna said in Sunday school. "I knew I had to begin reading more, listening to those around me, and interpreting facts, so I could provide the best guidance for him. Parenting is such a big responsibility."

These questions will help you determine if manipulation is present in your family:

- Is one person in the family making unnecessary demands on others? (Parent to child, child to parent.)
- Does one person often try to make a deal with another, such as "I will do this for you if will you do this for me?"
- Is the parent trying to live through the child, such as the case when the parent says, "I never had piano lessons; therefore, you will take them—like it or not!"
- Are expectations unrealistic, such as, do the parents expect outstanding work from an average child?
- Are nonverbal forms of manipulation being used, such as pouting, moodiness, holding back on conversation or affection, or indifference?

Manipulation occurs in most families. Most of us are guilty of either trying to be in constant control or letting ourselves be controlled by those around us. While one person may win through this method of relating to others, it can turn a genuine, honest relationship into one of game-playing, mistrust, and deceit. Through being open and honest in our relationships, we can change controlling situations into situations of give-and-take, compromise, and genuine caring.

"When conflict occurs, is quitting the best solution? Does quitting really help to make peace? Is quitting part of our duty as Christians?"

 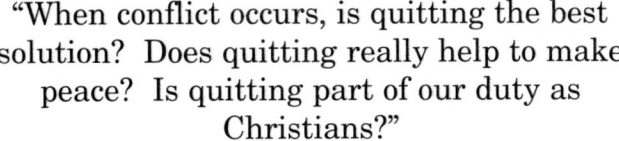

23

Peacemaker

"Blessed are the peacemakers, for they will be called sons of God."

—Matthew 5:9

"I quit!" My daughter Ashley screamed as her older brother and sister began to take the lead in the Monopoly game.

"I quit." These two powerful words are spoken in moments of intense anger by both young and old. As a young child, like Ashley, we learn that quitting can remove us from uncomfortable situations. If there was unfairness in the game we were playing, we could just quit. If two friends conspired against us at the park, we could always leave.

What about real life? When conflict occurs, is quitting the best solution? Does quitting really help to make peace? Is quitting part of our duty as Christians?

Conflict may be defined as a sharp disagreement or opposition, as of interests, ideas, and so forth. And even the most vibrant and caring Christians experience conflict from time to time. Sometimes this strife is between husband and wife, resulting in separation or divorce. Sometimes it's in the workplace, resulting in one person's leaving the job. And sometimes it's in the church, resulting in members leaving the church.

Conflict that gets out of hand can be devastating. For example, my friend Susan couldn't resolve the conflict she had experienced at her office. She told of being so angry she was ready to quit her job. She said that her nine staff members had not received their annual bonuses because company profits were down.

"It's just not fair," Susan said to the small group of Christians in my home. "I received my bonus because I'm the office manager, but the others got nothing. We're talking about people who were counting on this for their children's Christmas presents. I'm determined to help them get what they have earned or I am going to quit this company."

On the other hand, her husband Bill had a different opinion. He wanted Susan to gloss over the situation without resolving the conflict. "I don't think you should rock the boat," he said sternly. "Just do your work and don't worry about your staff. It's not your fault if they are being treated unfairly. Blame the national office. After all, your career could be jeopardized if you say anything."

Conflict, differences, is nothing new. The Early Church faced it, not only from the outside but also from within. But the Apostle Paul affirmed the unity of Christians in Romans 12:5: "We who are many form one body."

As my husband and I have served many churches, we have experienced that not only are people in each church different, but even groups of Christians within the church differ. Within each local church are individuals and groups of people who practice the Christian faith in a variety of ways.

Paul was well aware of this diversity in the church. He saw Christians with different gifts: prophecy, service, teaching, exhortation, giving, and acting with mercy (Romans 12:6–7). He saw a church with different offices and functions: apostles, prophets, evangelists, pastors, and teachers (Ephesians 4:11). To his distress, Paul also noticed the rise of divisiveness: "I follow Paul . . . I follow Apollos . . . I follow Cephas . . . I follow Christ" (1 Corinthians 1:12).

Yet Paul insisted that the Church of Jesus Christ is one whole body. Like the human body, it needs different kinds of members—feet, hands, ears, eyes. The Church is defined by its unity, not its diversity. That's the beauty of our faith!

What about in day-to-day living? Do you experience situations in your daily living where you have to seek unity by resolving conflict? Sometimes in the middle of family or job or church conflict, you are forced to determine if you are going to be an appeaser or a peacemaker.

You may have tried to solve a disagreement by appeasement, giving in to keep peace, saying, "Oh, yes, you are absolutely right," even though you really felt the person's opinion was very wrong. Or you may have kept some of the facts out of the discussion in order to avoid conflict. Some of us even hide the truth by ignoring the question at hand. Why ask for trouble?

Look at the following statements about conflict. How do you usually respond?

When I see people in conflict, I . . .

- Tell them to knock it off
- Try to make them feel at ease so they will stop fighting
- Help them understand each other's point of view
- Let someone else handle it
- Try to decide exactly who started the argument and blame the conflict on that person
- Try to work out a compromise so everyone will end up smiling
- Turn the situation into a joke
- Tell them to stop making a fuss over nothing
- Make one person give in and apologize, even though I really don't know who is at fault
- Try to divert attention from the conflict by changing the subject abruptly
- Ignore it and hope it will go away
- Threaten to tell someone else if they don't calm down
- Threaten to leave if a peaceful decision can't be reached
- Pray about it and hope God hears quickly

We have many ways of dealing with conflict. One great challenge of being a Christian is in times of conflict to choose to make peace with those around us. But there is a difference between making peace and offering appeasement.

An appeaser avoids the issue, resorting to any technique to ease the conflict. Such avoidance, however, satisfies the opponents only temporarily; their conflict will probably return. As for the appeaser himself, he may compromise his values, ideas, or morals just to make those in conflict happy. Often an appeaser is one who quits those situations that create conflict in his own life, feeling this will solve the problem.

A peacemaker on the other hand seeks to resolve conflict. He chooses to hear all sides of the problem and searches for the truth. This search involves listening, weighing the arguments, and taking a stand—even one that may not be popular. But being a peacemaker is a risk. Someone is sure to become angry when his view is challenged. Being a peacemaker, however, is part of our challenge as Christ's disciples.

Jesus Christ was a peacemaker. He was not concerned with winning a popularity contest. As He sought to share God's love and principles of fairness and equality, He made many enemies of people who preferred rather the status quo.

Many people have lost tolerance for conflict, as headlines often indicate. The turmoil and unrest in Panama and Romania in recent years have shown that sometimes this conflict is a by-product of peacemaking and will occur when people are being tyrannized and oppressed. At the same time, these countries have also proven that peacemaking can result in reconciliation, as the oil of peace is poured into the troubled waters of conflict.

Going that extra mile to be a peacemaker in our family, church, and community can be a risk. As we seek the truth in situations of conflict, we risk being disliked by some people. And when as a peacemaker, we take a stand—especially an unpopular stand—we may be ostracized by our friends or loved ones. Consequently, teaching children to be advocates of issues and circumstances they know to be true presents a challenge. As peacemakers, we see what we are inviting into their lives. Nevertheless, we need to pass on to them the role of peacemaker. What are the benefits? We experience cooperation and our children learn to work together and trust each other. As peacemakers, we communicate with one another and our children learn to listen with compassion and sensitivity to each other. As Christians making peace, we become tolerant, and our children learn to respect each other's views and differences and work together for the best solution.

With an extra effort to carry peace into conflict situations, we can become peacemakers at home, at church, and at work. Our influence can become a world of peace as we fulfill the words of Jesus: "Blessed are the peacemakers, for they will be called the sons of God" (Matthew 5:9).

24

The Power of Touch

"[Jesus] took the children in his arms, put his hands on them and blessed them."
—Mark 10:16

Recently I took twenty children from our church to a local nursing home to entertain the residents with a clown ministry performance. After we arrived, the brightly dressed youngsters sang their medley of songs, then proceeded to greet our elderly hosts.

As the line of children walked by one woman, she reached out and grabbed the hand of my youngest daughter. I heard her ask in a feeble voice, "May I touch your hand, sweetheart?"

Young Ashley looked up at me in surprise at her strange request, then hesitantly sat down beside her wheelchair as the woman's soft wrinkled hand touched my child's smooth skin.

Now that may seem like an unusual request for some, especially in a world where touch has become frowned upon, but it does point out a most needed form of communication.

Think about it. Isn't it appealing to hug someone we know well and care about? Cuddling a helpless newborn or a wide-eyed toddler is easy. Yet most of us find it difficult to embrace the unlovely, the rebellious, the aged, the diseased—those who need physical assurance the most. Physical affection is a basic human need. Psychological research confirms this fact again and again, claiming that children must have this touching to grow up secure—or even to survive.

"Hugs are the best form of emotional and physical therapy," claims Jo Lindberg, founder of Hugs for Health Foundation. Embraces provide lots of physical contact, which has a healing power. Research reveals that touching can help lower high blood pressure and cholesterol, regulate the heartbeat, strengthen the immune system, even lull hyperactive children.

"Parents hug and kiss their children but forget that they need cuddles, too," notes Lindberg. "Ask your kids for hugs; you'll feel good." Dr. Lindberg prescribes four hugs a day for survival, eight for maintenance, and twelve for growth ("Your Health," *Redbook Magazine*, September 1993, 48).

In His ministry, Jesus expressed concern for people and healed many people through the use of His hands. For example, after receiving the little children over the objections of His disciples, Jesus "took the children in his arms, put his hands on them and blessed them" (Mark 10:16). When Peter's mother-in-law was ill, Jesus "touched her hand and the fever left her" (Matthew 8:15).

We easily visualize our Lord putting His arms around children, lifting up the lame, and embracing those in pain. As He preached love and concern, He also demonstrated them: He reached out with gentle, caring hands, touching cold and empty lives with His power.

Many times people in our families or neighborhoods are lonely or need a gentle stroke, a supportive hug, or someone to hold their hands. Shut-ins and other elderly persons need the support and assurance that only a warm touch can provide. Anger or hostility in children or teenagers can sometimes be alleviated with a warm, caring embrace.

A counselor said, "I was talking with a mother and her daughter recently. I asked the mother if her daughter loved her, and she replied, 'Oh, certainly.' Then, I asked the young teen if her mother loved her, to which she said, 'No, she doesn't.' The mother was shocked and said, 'I tell you I love you every day.' But the teen said sadly, 'You never hug me. . . .'"

Unfortunately, because of physical abuse of one kind or another, we have become a hands-off society. Yet the needs for positive strokes still remains. A pat on the shoulder, a hug, or a loving back rub are often just as appreciated as saying the words "I love you."

Touch can also be a preventive medicine. Parents generous with hugs and kind words secure their children against peer pressure.

Several years ago, at a youth conference, I heard about a study at a large northwestern university which affirmed this mysterious power of touch. A number of young adults who checked out books at the library were given a handshake, a pat on the arm, or other touch by the staff librarians. After leaving the building, each student was questioned about his library. Of the students who had been touched, 100 percent reported positive feelings. Those who were not touched had either apathetic or negative feelings.

If such limited contact can make a difference in someone's attitude about a library, think of the difference touch can make in our homes! Using this nonverbal form of communication allows you to interact with all members of your family in an equally positive way. They may be hiding behind masks or feeling insecure. Your caring touch can express acceptance, and encourage openness and communication.

Often a loving touch enables you to be sensitive in situations where words seem out of place. You can do this by offering those extra touches and hugs even when the person is not too lovable. A pat on the shoulder, a hug, a firm handshake, or other kinds of touches usually generate a stronger sense of caring and concern than spoken words. This touching breaks down barriers, saying, "I care about you."

A familiar bumper sticker asks, "Have you hugged your kid today?" But let's not stop there; let's include the aged, friends, coworkers, and even enemies in the touches we give. It is time to reach out and start touching again. Maybe in doing so, we can embrace our families and others and create a more peaceful and caring world for them. Through this simple gift, we can help alleviate more than a little bit of loneliness in the world.

25

Giving Up Free Agency

"Choose for yourselves this day whom you will serve."
—Joshua 24:15

Your fourteen-year-old teen has just been invited to go to the mountains on a big skiing trip with some close friends. He has never seen snow before and the thought of skiing for the first time is exciting. At the last minute, you remember that he agreed to help with the youth Christmas pageant at your church that same week. The minister said they are really counting on him to accompany the musical with his guitar. Which choice does he make?

Your high school daughter promised your neighbors that she would house-sit during the month of August so they could take that cruise they have been wanting to take for years. Then in early August she receives a phone call telling of a big weekend reunion of some school friends at a beach resort upstate. Both commitments are at the same time. "We know this is last minute, but we hope you will come," the friends from school plead. Which commitment does she keep?

Does your child make decisions and stick to them, or does he play the free agent, keeping his options open? At one time professional athletes were traded by owners of teams; then came free agency, an athlete was free to choose, to keep his options open until he got an offer that appealed to him. Instead of having to go with the team of his owner's choice, the athlete could make his own deal and sign with whomever he chose. With us it's a way of not making a commitment, not obligating ourselves to any person, task, or group. Playing the free agent is often beneficial at the moment; it allows one the freedom to pick and choose—to do what one wants when one wants.

Children learn how to play the free agent from adults. In fact, most adults play the free agent every day of their lives. The motivating factor may be selfishness; the motivating factor may be fear. For example, perhaps they are afraid of making a decision that would cause undue embarrassment or unhappiness. Making the wrong choice, such as in a career change or a financial investment, could result in anxiety or rejection by family and loved ones. Some adults fear failure and for that reason never launch out, never making a firm decision. So they learn to depend on others to make their decisions.

Sarah, the mother of two preschool boys, experienced this fear recently. "When my husband lost his job, I knew I should go back to work," she admitted. "Yet I was torn between leaving the boys all day and staying home with them. I became anxious and frustrated because I knew I had a decision to make and just didn't know how."

After finishing college, Rick chose to work from the home so his wife could complete her degree. He sees clients and cares for their toddler, Mandy, while maintaining the household. "I still can't accept my choice. Even though I enjoy being with Mandy, I keep hurrying my wife in her studies so I can move back into the business world. I don't feel comfortable with any choices right now."

People also keep their options open out of selfishness. For example, in the business world, the free agent is rampant, with people constantly changing jobs and careers while searching for that magic slot that will ensure happiness. Pastors are faced with these free agents in the local church, people who hesitate to join the congregation because they prefer their independence. Unfortunately a family can suffer the selfishness of keeping one's options open. Some people marry with the thought in mind that if it doesn't work out, if they ever sense disillusionment or dissatisfaction, they can always get a divorce. Children learn to hold out for immediate gratification, wearing down parents who cannot teach them to make responsible decisions.

The gravest danger of becoming a free agent, playing the options game, is seen in the hazards it creates for our children. Family units break down as commitment diminishes; parents become indifferent to their relationships. Morals and values are weakened when a firm stand for them is not taken; children are unsure of what is right or wrong.

Generally, playing the free agent in a family results in stunted growth of the members. If you don't take responsibility, you will become irresponsible. If you make few commitments, you will become flighty and uncommitted. Most unfortunate, you lose strength of character as you are seen as being undependable.

Jesus' ministry was one of calling people to commit themselves. As He confronted people in different situations, He encouraged them to choose between good and evil. The uniqueness of the New Testament lies in this new strength to choose, to break out of the bondage of sin.

As Christian parents, God calls us to be obedient in our newfound freedom to choose, our free agency. This summons involves our taking responsibility to act, to commit ourselves to the good. And by taking action and making such commitments, we will role model selflessness and responsibility before our watching children.

You can begin making commitments by setting your priorities straight, for example, God, family, self, career. By setting clear goals for yourself and your family, you will see your obligations as an important part of your life. Ask, What do I want to commit myself to? How can I best serve God in the family? church? community? How much family time is needed? How much personal time is needed?

Becoming a committed person also involves making wise decisions. Weigh the options that involve your personal priorities and goals. Ask, What are the pros and cons of each alternative? In making the choice, it is important that the alternatives are prayerfully and carefully considered. Allow time to talk with other people and listen to their experiences. Growth will occur as God speaks to you through others, in prayer, and through the Scriptures.

Select the best alternative and launch out in faith that God will support you. Making a decision and putting your life in forward motion includes risking that God will protect you AND catch you if you should fall. If you fail, evaluate your commitment. Ask, What went wrong? Why didn't the choice work? What circumstances could have made it better? By evaluating the decision and your commitment, you gain insight into who you are, and through this self-evaluation you are able to mature in your decision making.

As you drop your free agency, letting go your options, committing yourself to God, you will begin to see a change in yourself. Strength of character will increase as you become dependable, and responsibility will multiply as you begin to fulfill obligations. As you begin to really lean on God for support when you make decisions and commitments, faith becomes more than just a Sunday morning word. However, the big reward you will see as you make firm commitments is the by-product of committed children, children willing to make decisions and stick to them.

Are you a free agent? Or do you live a life of commitment and responsible decision-making? Remember, the free agent makes an irresponsible and selfish member of the body of Christ, and a loser in responsible Christian living.

It's your decision!

26

Accepting Differences

"Accept one another, then, just as Christ accepted you, in order to bring praise to God."

—Romans 15:7

When our youngest daughter Ashley was three years old, she was diagnosed as having amblyopia, or *lazy eye*. The treatment? Ashley had to wear an eye patch over the normal eye and corrective glasses during the daytime for three-years. This forced the "lazy" eye and the brain to begin working together.

The reaction of people around Ashley startled us.

"What's wrong with her eye? Why does she have a Band-Aid on it?" asked a well-meaning friend at her child's birthday party in front of Ashley and all of her peers.

Another acquaintance mentioned that "Once you get that eye problem straightened out, she will be a beautiful young girl." (We thought she was beautiful just the way she was!)

"Is something wrong with me, Mommy?" she asked one night at bedtime. "Everyone stares at my eye patch." It was true. We observed that when Ashley wore the patch, no adult or child really felt comfortable around her. It was as if a patch over her eye suddenly changed her into a different person.

What about in your family? Are you teaching your children how to deal with people who may look, act, or talk differently? Do your children immediately accept everyone as part of God's world, or do they isolate the person by ignoring him, gossiping about his disability, or shying away out of fear? Does your child see a disability as an inconvenience that must be accepted, or does he choose not to associate with people who are less than perfect?

Even many adults don't know how to approach someone with a physical disability. And if adults don't know how to approach such a person, how can we teach our children?

The types of disabilities people can have are endless. Ashley's disability (which is quite common in young children) forced her to wear an eye patch to preschool and at play. A family friend, Sarah, must stay in a wheelchair; she has muscular dystrophy. Other disabilities that are not quite as debilitating and affect most of us require small devices, such as glasses or hearing aids, to allow a normal life. Still other disabilities, such as a learning problem or a slight neurological disorder, are not even noticeable.

Many national disability organizations have made the public aware that certain terms are counterproductive. *Handicapped* is one such word. *The retarded* is another. Phrases such as "She is a cripple" or "He is a victim of . . . " are considered a disservice to the individual. They suggest using the term *disability,* and using it in conjunction with *people*, for example, *people who are disabled,* or being even more specific and saying *a person who has cerebral palsy.* Terms, such as *the disabled*, are not to be used as a generic reference to a group. It is recommended that the focus be on the person, instead of allowing the disability to overshadow the person.

Disabilities Your Child Might Encounter

Let's consider some common disabilities, which your child might encounter in meeting people each day at school or play.

Orthopedic Disabilities (bone and muscle problems). These disabilities include cerebral palsy, spina bifida, missing limbs, and spinal cord injuries producing paralysis. These can be caused by disease, accident, or merely birth (for example, premature birth).

Visually Impaired. A partially sighted person is one who has vision between 20/70 and 20/200. These people require enlarged printed material. A blind person has a vision of 20/200 or less.

Hearing Impaired. Loss of hearing may range from mild to profound and can affect one ear or both. Even with the use of aids, the hearing is distorted.

Mental Disability. Mental disability, according to the Federal Rehabilitation Act (Section 504), refers to four categories: psychiatric disability, retardation, learning disability, and (physical) head trauma, all of which impair to one degree or another the cognitive powers of an individual.

Learning Disabilities. A learning disability occurs when the brain does not properly interpret through the senses. Such disabilities include visual perception problems and auditory perception problems. Learning disabilities are neurological disorders that should not be confused with developmental disabilities.

Small/Short Stature. Do not refer to a person as a midget or a dwarf. Speak of that person as being *of small (or short) stature*. Some groups prefer *little people*; some do not.

Communicate with Your Child

The more acquainted your child is with disabilities, the more accepting he can become as he meets people at school, church, or play who are disabled. Look at the following steps to see how your child can become more aware and accepting.

Talk Openly About Being Disabled

Aware of the whispered comments and questions about Ashley's eye patch among the children at preschool, the teacher gathered Ashley's class during a sharing time, and I explained that Ashley's left eye was not working as well as her right one. I showed them the eye patch that she had to wear and gave each young child one to try on. The preschoolers stuck the patch on one eye and glared out with the other one.

"This isn't too bad," one youngster said as he walked around the room.

"Yeah," another child added. "It is just a little bit sticky."

This one time of openness among Ashley's peers ended the curiosity about her eye patch. After that day, no more was said.

Look around in your church and community. In our congregation several members use canes to assist them in walking.

Another young girl has cerebral palsy and must use a wheelchair and neck brace. A disability can come into a person's life at birth or later; in either case, the person should be accepted. Some of these people are challenged physically by an environment for the nondisabled. We are becoming more aware of that, so sidewalks, buildings, rest rooms, accommodate people who use wheelchairs.

If your child has questions about someone's disability, encourage him to ask you about the concern. Most individuals with disabilities want to be known as people first, so the child needs to relate to them in a normal way. Drawing attention to the disability should be avoided unless the person who has the disability brings it up. If your child is empathetic and the communication is open toward the other, caring can take place. Have your child ask himself, *How would I feel if it were me? What problems would I face? What limits would I have in my life? How would I want to be treated?* Encourage your child to obey Christ's command to be loving and kind to all God's children. It is also important for your child to see the common interests he may have with the person who is disabled instead of the differences. Everyone has abilities and your child can learn to encourage or focus on these in others.

Obtain Books on the Disabled

Your public library is an excellent resource for finding books that focus on people with disabilities in a positive way. Often we get the impression that a disability lessens the person. Correct this by providing books for your child that show people with disabilities leading successful and productive lives. You can point out that our country had a president who had a disability: Franklin D. Roosevelt had polio, and he served the most terms as president in the history of our country. Stephen Hawking, prize-winning physicist, uses a wheelchair. A book about Joni Eareckson Tada may inspire you. Her tremendous faith and persistence in living for the Lord after a diving accident made her a quadriplegic is an inspiration to many.

Being aware of people with special abilities also enables your child to see and be thankful for the many God-given talents he has.

Invite Persons with Disabilities to Speak at Your Church

A woman who is blind is a member of our congregation. She is a brilliant scholar and impresses everyone she meets. The children in our church accept her without any apparent awareness of her impairment. Asking her to speak to a children's group proved beneficial. The funny incidents she shared about her life in a dark world broke the ice and encouraged the children to ask her questions that normally wouldn't be asked.

Getting to know those with disabilities personally is indispensable. A trip to a nursing home with a school club or to a rehabilitation center with some friends could help your child become more understanding and accepting. Many church groups take on service projects as they work with people having disabilities, helping them to live life to the fullest.

Experience What It Would Be Like to Be Disabled

After Ashley's classmates put on the eye patches, they never mentioned this to her again. What was once a mystery was now understood, and the children realized Ashley had not changed.

Have your child take a rubber band and stretch it around his fingers. Now ask him to try to write his name or start a homework assignment. This is what many people with disabilities have to tolerate if they have severe arthritis, cerebral palsy, or other neurological or joint diseases.

Tie a handkerchief around your child's eyes so he can't see. Ask him to try to walk around his bedroom carefully. Did he bump into anything? Does he know where the bed is? Visually impaired people have to cope with their environment in this way every day of their lives.

Encourage your child to imagine living his daily life without the use of legs or even arms. Many disabled people have lost the use of their limbs and have to compensate for this loss by holding things in their teeth.

At lunch on her first day back at King High, Sarah, a wheelchair-user, moved from her chair to the bench in the cafeteria with the help of some old friends. She then let these curious friends get in her wheelchair and try to maneuver it through the crowd of students.

"Unbelievable," Rob said under his breath as he struggled to make the chair go forward and turn the corner. "There is no way I could make this chair work." The other teens agreed as they bumped into people and cafeteria tables.

Sarah sat back and laughed; her friends could barely make the wheelchair budge. More importantly, her friends were learning respect for Sarah's strength in overcoming her physical disability and living confidently in God's world.

Teaching your child to relax around persons who have disabilities and to treat these brothers and sisters with respect is very important. Your child will not know prejudice against anyone who is different if you teach understanding, compassion, and acceptance of all God's children.

27

Avoiding Burnout

"The Lord is my strength and my song."

—Exodus 15:2

We've all been there—feeling burned out from our duties as parents. We find that we are putting more and more time into our family life but enjoying it less. We realize that we have been giving negative rather than positive attention to our children, failing to enjoy their special personalities.

Is your parenting attitude full of apathy and resentment as you juggle too many outside activities or a career along with rearing children? Is being a parent in the nineties becoming overwhelming, leaving you tired and drained of enthusiasm?

If your answer is yes, you may be experiencing the pain of parent burnout.

Burnout is a state of physical and emotional exhaustion that is quite common among care givers, persons who are constantly nurturing others. Ministers, nurses, physicians, social workers, and caring parents are usually the victims of burnout.

My neighbor Sharon, a young mother of twins, said, "When Rob had to take a part-time job, along with his full-time job, I had to accept all of the household duties. Now I find myself so tired at night I can't wait for the children's bedtime. I hardly enjoy our family because I am always drained."

Feeling drained like Sharon is a major symptom of burnout. Another friend spoke of being uptight around his children. "I began to resent the little annoyances that occur all the time—the giggling during supper, asking for another glass of water at bedtime, and the constant questions," Richard said honestly. "I often feel overworked and under-appreciated, and sometimes I even resent my family."

Other typical symptoms of burnout include:
- Negative and rigid attitudes
- Dread of starting a new day
- Difficulty in sleeping
- Irritability and bursts of anger
- Lack of energy or enthusiasm
- Feelings of being overwhelmed

Burnout—A Vicious Cycle

Parents face many problems in rearing children in the nineties. First, the child may sense the parent's lack of control and interest and reflect it by becoming apathetic or uncontrollable. Thus, the entire family becomes engaged in a vicious cycle. The parent blames the child for poor behavior. The child, in turn, blames the parent for negative treatment. In the more advanced cases of parent burnout, the weary, confused adult simply quits caring—leaving the child to basically rear him or herself.

Most parents experience burnout at some time or another. Single parents are highly susceptible if they carry the burden of rearing the children alone. Homes where both parents have active careers feel this pressure as quality family time is limited. Burnout is also rampant in homes where one adult stays at home full time. Wherever there is a child to nurture, there is *constant* responsibility for that child. Most caring parents can become so consumed with that responsibility that they begin to resent their duties. When this resentment and apathy occur, burnout takes its toll.

But burnout doesn't have to result in quitting. If the symptoms are sighted early, the vicious cycle can be stopped.

Psychologists advise persons confronted with burnout to listen to the warning signs from the body. Signs of stress such as rapid heartbeat, stomachaches, headaches, or other bodily symptoms can alert you that something is amiss. Once aware of these symptoms and the fact that the body is under pressure, you can begin to evaluate your obligations and pace yourself in your family life.

Verbalize Feelings

First, evaluate your personal feelings. Talk with your spouse or a close friend about the pressures of being a parent. Nothing can be clearly understood without open discussion. Realize that negative feelings are normal. No relationship is immune to resentment or anger.

John, a small business owner and father of three teens, feels confident that it is important to express negative feelings in an appropriate manner. "I have found it necessary to identify the emotions and what triggers the anger inside me," he said. "If a family member has been slack in fulfilling his responsibility, I try to talk it out before an explosion occurs. Once I identify the initial cause of anger, anxiety, or resentment, I can begin to handle these feelings without hurting anyone."

Set Worthy Goals

Setting goals is vital for avoiding and overcoming parent burnout. Because of society's pressures, we may try to become a "super parent." I overheard several women talking at a local school meeting. Each one seemed to outdo the other with claims of having the "perfect" child. Parents feel pressured to compete with everyone for the most talented, most intelligent, most well-adjusted child. Yet in the midst of our struggle, we need to set priorities in our use of time and we need to set realistic goals that make a difference. Do we give family worship priority in our home, or is the popular TV show occupying that time? Is church attendance a family affair, or do we find ourselves too tired to attend after Saturday's outing?

A pastor said, "Parents in the nineties must prioritize their goals. By doing so, they will find unimportant activities may not be necessary. The main priority in the lives of Christian families must be God and His Church. Only then will families begin to experience an inner peace that can help heal burnout."

Care for One's Own Needs

To remember that one is a person first and a parent second is also important in curing burnout. We cheat our children if we ignore our own personal needs. We have been given the great commandment in the Gospels, "Love your neighbors as yourself" (Mark 12:31). This verse presupposes that we love ourselves. If we are full of personal tensions and anxieties, perhaps we are not loving ourselves enough. Unless we care for ourselves, we may not be adequate to love and care for our children.

Use Baby-Sitters

Baby-sitters can take over when the pressures of parenting begin to overwhelm us. An older couple may enjoy (or at least agree to) being substitute grandparents so a couple can take a weekend for renewal. A high-school student may enjoy a chance to become a close friend with our children as we get away for an evening. Interview these sitters and make sure their values and methods of discipline are appropriate. Then keep their telephone numbers handy and use them as needed to keep your role of parent from becoming overwhelming.

Divide Chores

To alleviate the mounting parenting pressure, assign all family members household responsibilities. The children can help decide how the chores should be distributed and become part of the family routine. Parents can outline the specific tasks and how they are to be done so the family can continue to run smoothly.

We need to realize that when we assign household chores to younger children, the task may not be done as we would do it. But by letting the children help, we can have more time for enjoying the children and for building relationships.

Use Support Groups

Many Christians depend on church support groups to feel recharged after symptoms of burnout. Jana, the leader of a small support group, tells of members finding hope when they are able to discuss family problems with other concerned Christians.

"Most churches are usually enthusiastic in helping to start parent support groups," she said. "Curriculum can be studied to enrich family life as parents learn to deal effectively with discipline and time management problems. Bible studies can help overextended fathers and mothers to have hope when they seem so defeated. Praying with other Christians gives strength to all members as they leave to tackle the awesome responsibility of rearing children."

Wanda, a member of this support group, said, "Parents should not hesitate in sharing personal frustrations in these Christian fellowship groups. Many have found answers and relief as they carefully and prayerfully discuss their home situations. I know I have!"

The minister of your church is an excellent resource for support and guidance in overcoming burnout. If your family problems are too intense, your pastor can recommend professional help. If the situation is temporary, he or she can direct you toward attainable goals that can help during the crucial time.

Have Family Worship

Most important, we can lead our families in home worship and Bible study. This time of spiritual oneness with God and with one another can keep communication open. Problems can be shared, changes can be planned, and improvements can be made within the home to relieve some of the parenting pressure. Families should discuss modes of discipline and set limits within the family. Children should be encouraged to participate.

Let's evaluate our role as Christian parents. Are we pacing our efforts as we serve God? Or do we resent the energy we expend in our families, not realizing that perhaps we are heading toward parenting burnout?

Being a parent involves setting realistic goals, opening up with personal problems, and taking time to recharge our personal lives periodically. All of these survival tips can help us to avoid parent burnout.

"Unless we care for ourselves, we may not be adequate to love and care for our children."

28

Leave the Label Off

"'The Lord does not look at the things man looks at. Man looks at the outward appearance, but the Lord looks at the heart.'"

—1 Samuel 16:7

I knew there was a problem when Brittnye came home from school several months ago; I could see she had been crying.

Over a plate of chocolate chip cookies later, she began to talk. "I don't get it, Mom," she said. "I got the highest grade on the ninth-grade biology test. Instead of congratulating me, some of my best friends started calling me 'teacher's pet.'"

Between bites she continued to express her feelings: "I work hard to obey the teacher and make good grades in class, but then the kids start calling me names. But if I didn't obey the teacher, I'd be in trouble like the rest of the kids in my class."

I ached for my daughter who was hurting so, for I knew what she was feeling. It is difficult to stand up for what you believe and take abuse for it. For Brittnye, being the odd one in class made life miserable. Her values, things she believed in, were being challenged by her peers. Usually children attack the person who's different—whether it's a physical or an intellectual difference—attaching painful nicknames to that person.

Several days later, I was running at a track near a local junior high school with my son. I overheard a group of elementary school boys yelling and jeering as a chubby teen in front of us slowly jogged the final turn on the outdoor track. "Get the lead out, 'Slowpoke'!" the boys screamed. My heart went out to him. The incident brought back old memories: In my own elementary school class, a boy who had been different was stuck with the name "Slowpoke" by classmates. His name was Donald. Because of a slight physical disability from birth, his movements were not quite as fast as the other children's. I clearly remember the day he ran the track in physical education class with tears streaming down his face as insensitive peers yelled cruel remarks such as "Make those legs work, Slowpoke!" I empathized with him and was determined to be his friend.

As I got to know Donald at school and at his home, I realized that this physically slow boy was definitely not slow intellectually. Throughout his room was a collection of intricate models, from rockets to the earliest biplane. Besides having constructed them, he was extremely knowledgeable about the actual planes themselves. He would explain in detail the smallest part. According to Donald, each component of the plane was essential, no matter how minor it appeared.

As Donald described the designs of the newer models, I remember thinking how cruel our elementary school friends were for labeling him slow, as somehow being inferior because of his physical disability. At a very young age, I was shown by my friend Donald how each person is indispensable and how appearances tell little of what someone really is.

My family moved a few years later to a nearby community, and Donald and I lost touch throughout the remaining school years. But when high school graduation came, I read in our local newspaper that Donald had won the state merit scholarship and was to attend an Ivy League college.

Ten years later, I traveled back to my small home town to visit relatives; an aunt showed me another clipping out of the city's newspaper with a large picture captioned "Local Man Selected Designer." It was Donald, sitting at a huge design board; in the background, pictures of aircrafts, shuttles, and missiles decorated the walls of his office at the aeronautics center. Donald had realized his dream of putting together those vital parts to create an efficient airplane. Donald had proven that "Slowpoke" was a very misleading label.

Is your child sometimes ostracized by his peers? Many children experience this feeling of rejection as they pass through stages of childhood or adolescence. Perhaps your child has been labeled "bossy" or "smarty" by peers because of some difference. These labels are not always meant to be derogatory. Most of the time a label is developed out of the habit of referring to a person by what is perceived as a dominant trait. However, the unfortunate part of giving anyone such a label is that after many years of growth and development, the label is often no longer true. The eight-year-old girl nicknamed "fatty" becomes the graceful, slender model in college. The boy who was called "jock" and encouraged only in athletics while in junior high school becomes the class valedictorian with computers as his main interest.

The biggest problem with giving a child a label is that it can hinder growth. A child who is constantly referred to as "spacy" may feel that she has to be that way. Another child who has been titled "sloppy" may accept that nickname as an excuse for his behavior or a forecast of his potential. A label can clearly be an obstacle for a child.

Even if families become aware of the hazards of labeling a child, other people, including well-meaning teachers and friends, often typecast the child, telling others that the shy boy is "a sissy" or "unmotivated." Once a label is attached, it takes a great deal of effort to tear it off.

A friend said she was shocked that she was accepted into a master's program at a well-known university. "I was always the one my teachers thought was not studious," she exclaimed. "My older sister, who chose not to attend college, was always the academic achiever."

Things do change as we grow older and become more aware of our strengths and assets. Realizing that that happens, we can make living easier for our children and those around us by checking our tendency to label them, handing them, in effect, a self-fulfilling prophecy and hemming them in with a set of expectations.

Recently I overheard an older woman in our congregation reprimand my youngest child for "speaking too loud" in the vestibule of the sanctuary. I'll admit my reaction was one of shock as my daughter replied emphatically, "I'm not a preacher's kid—I am a normal kid."

Our goal as Christian parents should be to allow all children the opportunity to be a "normal kid," so they might be accepted instead of being singled out as different. We can do more than refrain from labeling our children; we can broaden their concept of who they are and what they can be. Being aware of the phases your child passes through and affording him opportunities for development can open doorways for discovering his potential.

29

Sarah on My Mind

"I thank my God every time I remember you."

—Philippians 1:3

 I don't know what made me sit down that rainy Tuesday morning and write that letter to Sarah, my friend of twenty years. But a persistent voice inside me kept saying her name over and over. As I finally responded and put pen to paper, I wondered why I would think of her suddenly when we hadn't seen each other in over fifteen years?

 Sarah Carter and her family were strong members of our church while my husband Bob was a seminary student in Atlanta, Georgia. For some reason, even though we were almost as young as some of their children, there was a special bond between the Carters and the Bruces. We spent many evenings visiting with them and sharing good times. When our first son, Rob, was born, Sarah and her children made a large banner that went across the front of the parsonage with the words "It's a boy!" painted on it. Their youngest son Ryan was in our youth group and sang in a traveling choral ensemble with us.

 Sarah and her family touched our lives in many ways those three short years. I especially remember one early December when the tires on our worn-out Chevy became equally worn out. "What will we do?" Bob had said to me that morning. "We don't have any extra money right now. How will I get to school tomorrow to take my exams?"

That day a check for $100 arrived in the mail with a note from Sarah and her family.

"This is what we are giving each child in our family for Christmas. You are like our children. Merry Christmas!"

How could she have known we needed $100 for tires?

Another evening that winter, Bob and I were homebound with the flu. We had the accompanying fever, coughing, and aches. Rob was just an infant. As we lay in bed trying to decide who would get up and feed the baby, the doorbell rang. There was Sarah and her children with a steaming pot of chicken soup.

"Thought this might help you get well," she said matter-of-factly. "And by the way, we're taking Rob to our house for a few days until you get back on your feet. This young man needs to be rocked and fed."

With that, her girls wrapped up our baby and put him in their car, relieving us of added responsibility while we were so ill.

Bob graduated from seminary and we accepted our first appointment in Florida. Somehow we lost touch with Sarah and her family. Through the years we exchanged a card or two; occasionally we received a newsy message through mutual friends.

That rainy Tuesday morning in Jacksonville, Sarah was on my mind in a powerful way. Writing letters is not something I enjoy doing, but I had to respond to this nudge. I sat by the fireplace in our den and wrote her a two-page letter telling her about our busy family—"Rob is now a student at Emory University, Brittnye is a junior in high school, and Ashley (you never met Ashley!) is now in seventh grade. Sarah, how quickly time flies." I found an old address book and wrote Sarah's address on the envelope, sealed it, then put it in the mailbox.

The next evening as I was getting ready for bed, the phone rang.

I heard my daughter in another room: "Mrs. Carter? Sure, my mom is here."

Mrs. Carter? Sarah Carter? I hurriedly picked up the phone. "Sarah? Is this really you?" I couldn't believe I was actually talking with this wonderful friend after all these years.

"Did you get my letter?" I didn't know how a letter could have been received so quickly, but surely that was why she was calling.

"A letter? Did you write me?" Sarah seemed surprised that I

had even thought of her. "No, I haven't seen any letter. We came to Jacksonville early this morning. My friend died here on Tuesday. I couldn't wait to give you a call while I was in town and try to catch up on the years."

Sarah went on to explain that her dear friend, Mary, lived in the same city as we did. Mary had died on Tuesday—the same day Sarah was on my mind, and the day I wrote the letter.

We talked and talked that night, catching up on old times. She proudly told me of the accomplishments of her five children—many were teachers, and her son, Ryan, was a physician and professor at Emory University—the very same school our son attended. She told about the recent sadness she had faced: her husband of fifty years was now in a nursing home with Alzheimer's disease, and her sister had died just a few months before.

"Debbie," she said, "this is a sad time in my life. I've lost my three best friends this year—my husband, my sister, and now Mary."

Is that why God had suddenly put Sarah on my mind? Is that why I felt so compelled to reach out to her yesterday?

"Oh, but Sarah," I said through my tears, "you have been blessed with so many more friends, too." I promised to keep in close touch with my friend from past years.

As I hung up the phone, I remembered the Scripture, "Little children, let us stop just saying we love people; let us really love them, and show it by our actions" (1 John 3:18 *Living Bible*). I thanked God that I had followed my thoughts and written the letter yesterday.

Unable to sleep that night, I reflected on what Sarah was going through in her times of sorrow. I felt comfort in knowing how God works in our lives: We are the hands and feet that respond when He calls us to care for those who are hurting. It was a truth I would try to bear in mind, especially when it came to remembering old friends.

"I felt comfort in knowing how God works in our lives: We are the hands and feet that respond when He calls us to care for those who are hurting."

30

How Do You Say It?

"Set an example . . . in speech, in life, in love, in faith and in purity."

—1 Timothy 4:12

"Come in the house right now. I mean it, young lady." I paused dramatically before each word as I commanded my young daughter to come inside. This was my way of showing strong parental authority and it usually had good results.

"Oh, Mommy," young Brittnye answered crying. "Just one more minute on my bike, puh-leaze!" Brittnye clasped her hands and pleaded as she spoke. She also had found a way of controlling those around her by changing the tone of her voice.

Are you aware of the attitudes you pass on to your family and friends by your tone of voice, that particular way of pitching the voice that expresses your meaning or feeling? The tone of your voice can be either helpful or detrimental to those around you. Several years ago, we became aware of how we manipulated or ignored one another in our family simply by how we spoke.

One day, after feeling quite misunderstood by my family, I really listened to how we each used voice inflections, syllable stress, and intensity in sound to manipulate one another. I admitted that I personally used voice control to get my own way. Did the other members of the family really do the same?

I listened to myself speak to the children. Instead of raising my voice to accurately express my anger, I spoke in a deep monotone and purposely held back all feeling as I commanded, "Get into your rooms and do not come out. Now!" Again, I left an intentional pause between each word for added effect.

Other times when I was confronted by a discussion that threatened me, I would not admit my true feelings. Instead, I commanded, "We will not discuss this anymore. The subject is now closed."

Interestingly, the manner in which I controlled the event by my tone of voice reflected my control-taking personality.

I listened cautiously to my husband, a minister, and found him to be quite the opposite of me. While he became vulnerable by exposing his genuine feelings, he often ignored "trivia talk," such as the leaky sink, the stopped-up shower, or the abundance of weeds in the backyard. I recalled the days of graduate school when he studied his textbooks. I would often talk aloud to the walls, poking fun at his inability to pay attention to any conversation that did not deal with theology.

Our three children are all products of their environment, each learning unique techniques of manipulating others through voice control. Rob, our oldest child, is always in a hurry. During my experiment when Rob was asked about school, he would quickly yell, "Oh, it was fine, Mom," as he ran out the door to meet his friends. Brittnye, our middle daughter, seemed to linger around to discuss even the pickiest item, yet always spoke with a whimper and whine. As she struggled to control her parents, she knew just the right way to cock her head and try to melt us with those brown eyes, and whisper, "Puh-leaze, Mommy. Just one more cookie, puh-leaze."

Ashley, our youngest child, had not yet formed a definite pattern of controlling us by her voice at that time, but we were beginning to see definite signals of control by the way she cried if not given her way.

One day, as a further part of my experiment, I clued my husband in on my project, and we listened to the attitudes we portrayed as we talked at dinner. Sure enough, Rob gulped down his food in a few seconds, stood up, and shouted, "Gotta go! Todd is going to show me how to throw a curve ball before dark. Good dinner, Mom." He barely finished the sentence as he slammed the door behind him. As usual, he spoke so quickly, he left no room for response.

As predicted, Brittnye played with her food until I was ready to clear the dishes from the table. As she toyed with the cold, green peas on her plate, she looked coyly up at her father and whimpered, "I really don't feel so well tonight. And just looking at those sick peas makes it much worse."

We said nothing to the children about our little project as we cleared the kitchen. Later that evening as we were all talking in the den before bedtime, I introduced what had been on my mind for the past few days.

"I don't always answer in a hurry," Rob defended himself immediately. "Listen . . . I . . . can . . . talk . . . slow. See?"

"I don't always whine, Mom. Do I, Dad?" Brittnye whimpered.

"Kids," Bob said as he faced the subject objectively. "It is not what you say, it's how you say it. Your mom and I are guilty also. How does Mom talk when she is angry or upset?"

"Very strict!" Brittnye yelled with new assurance.

"Very low and kinda scary," Rob added matter-of-factly.

"I don't always listen to you when you speak to me, right?" Bob questioned the two.

"Yeah, unless it is about church or soccer, huh, Dad?" Rob ribbed his dad.

"Well," I said with my usual control-taking voice. "What can we do about it? Can we change the way we talk to one another so others can better understand our true feelings?"

We thought for a moment. Then Rob decided that a tape of us discussing the subject would be fun. Bob agreed and set up the small recorder as we continued to talk. After fifteen minutes, we reran the tape and listened to the feedback.

"See, I sound pretty good," Rob bragged. "I'm not talking fast."

As the tape continued, I became threatened by a statement Bob made. I immediately went into my "full control" voice. Bob, in turn, had to be reminded twice to answer Brittnye's question, claiming he was thinking about his new worship schedule for next Sunday. Toward the end of the tape, Rob snapped that the experiment was boring and left to go to his room, and Brittnye whined that she was "tired."

"There we are. The proof is before you." I pointed to the innocent tape recorder. "The question is what are we going to do about the problem?"

We thought about the situation of trying to become more real as family members and less manipulative through our speech. Bob then opened the Bible and read several Scripture passages that helped us in revamping our habits. One Scripture verse that really spoke with authority is Colossians 4:6: "Let your conversation be always full of grace . . . so that you may know how to answer everyone."

Is speaking with forced self-control without showing any feeling or emotion really demonstrating that a person is full of God's grace? Is controlling people by whining or with hurried, flippant answers the type of speech God wants us to use? Is ignoring those you love a way of showing you care?

We evaluated our habits of speaking and even concluded that we had different ways of speaking to other people. "I guess I would never ignore a question, no matter what the subject, from a church member," Bob admitted frankly.

"Yeah. I talk to my friends a lot," Rob added. "I guess I'm just not in a hurry around them."

We had become more aware of a problem that strikes even the best of families. Our attitudes toward people often come across in not so much what we say, but how we say it.

We are still working on breaking these undesirable habits of communication. I am trying each day to speak in a normal voice when I am upset or angry, and am struggling to listen patiently to the ideas and opinions of my husband and children. Bob is making an effort to leave his work problems at church and tune in to the family while he is at home. We are both helping the three children work on their ways of controlling us by how they speak. Being congenial, being aware of those around us, and being genuine in our tones are three family goals we have set as we work to communicate more lovingly in our family.

31

Liberating the Juggler

"Blessed is the man who finds wisdom, the man who gains understanding."

—Proverbs 3:13

If you are a working mother who has both the option and the desire to stay home, read on. I, too, have worked outside the home while trying to raise three responsible children in a loving Christian home. I have impressed my employees and clients by being at work early and staying a bit late in order to add finishing touches to marketing projects. During the evening hours I have chaired PTO boards, lobbied for better school facilities, and have been homeroom mother for each child. And in the midst of career and civic duty, I have raised three independent children and have managed to stay happily married. But three weeks ago today, I gave it up.

I finally realized what my mother had been telling me for years, that this liberation that women struggle for in their homes and careers is more sizzle than substance. "If you were meant to be a juggler, I would have sent you to the circus to train," she said dryly during her last visit, before I rushed out the door carrying my youngest child's forgotten lunch box along with my leather briefcase. And that was in my left hand. My other arm served as a clothes rack for the shirts that had to go to the cleaners and the two pairs of shoes that were headed for the shoe repair shop. I ignored her comment as I rushed to the bank after dropping the lunch off at the elementary school, then raced to the printer to pick up my new business cards before getting to the office.

A juggler. The words blinked like a cursor in my mind as I sat in my office waiting for my first client. I keyboarded the words carefully into my computer and waited for the electronic brain to educate me.

"Juggler. noun. 1. a person who juggles; expert in sleight of hand; a person who practices trickery to deceive or cheat."

I quickly pressed the exit key as the words "trickery to deceive" caught my eye. Although I'm sure my mother meant "juggler" to be one who tries to do too many things at the same time, i.e., the expert in sleight of hand, in my situation I felt the term implied using trickery to cheat.

I tried to put the idea of being a juggler out of my mind while I spoke with various clients about their marketing needs that morning of my rebirth. But images of my responsibilities for that day kept haunting me. It was as if my mind was juggling the many tasks I had to do that afternoon in order to complete my day.

Let's see, my mind was racing, *meet Mom for lunch, write the press release for the grand opening, get the newsletter proof back from the printer, write a proposal for the new gift shop, set up appointments for advertising representatives to meet with shop owners,* and there was more. These thoughts were juggled with *Meet Ashley's bus at 3:10, remind Rob to take Ashley to tennis, pick up Brittnye from Student Council meeting, pick up milk for dinner, go by vet and get flea spray for dog, take shirts to cleaners, and have an early dinner so Rob can make it back to band practice—Oh, don't forget the education meeting at church to plan the teacher's appreciation luncheon.* And that was a calm day.

Enough! I felt my face as I dwelled on my many diverse responsibilities for the day: My cheeks were flushed. My heart was pounding as I kept thinking about all I had to do and the short time I had to do it in. *Make a list,* my inner self said. *Make a list and you can time yourself on each job. That way you can certainly get through your day on time.*

But the more I wrote on my list, the faster my heart seemed to pound. Each time I outlined a specific family responsibility, the phone would ring with inquiries and demands from my various clients. Instead of my list becoming more organized for the day, I was beginning to insert added tasks for the job. It began to look like this:

12:00—Meet Mom for lunch. Leave a bit early and go by the printer to get advertising spec. Return this to client by 1:30.

1:00—Have press releases prepared for afternoon delivery. Confirm all dates with client.

1:15—Write a note to remind Sunday school class students about the special guest next week.

1:30—Return advertising spec to client.

1:45—Stop by cleaners to take shirts.

2:00—Go by vet for flea powder.

2:15—Take newsletter proof back to printer. Be sure it is accurate because it's the final proof.

2:30—Drop off shoes at repair shop.

2:45—Stop by the house to call Bob and see how his day was. Walk the dog while there and pick up the mail.

3:00—Get to the bus stop before Ashley's bus comes so she feels secure.

And so on. As I looked at my list and the phone kept ringing, my face grew even more flushed and my heart pounded harder. *There,* I thought, *if I can stay on this tight schedule, I can get it all completed before I begin taking care of the kids at 3:00.*

But at 3:00, my hurried day of juggling career and family was genuinely taking its toll on my mind and body. "Mom," Ashley said insistently as she handed me her backpack stuffed with papers, "aren't you listening to me? I said I need pencils for school tomorrow."

And "Mom," my middle daughter reminded me as I picked her up from the meeting, "don't forget that we have to make brownies tonight for the party at school tomorrow."

And "Mom," my eldest son chimed as he jumped out of the van at the tennis courts, "don't forget to stop by the store and get the five-ring binder. I have to copy my physics notes tonight to turn in tomorrow."

Juggling? Liberated? I drove home from tennis lessons in silence, exhausted from the day—and this was only Monday.

When I got home at 5:30, my mother greeted me with "The

housekeeper called. She can't come tomorrow, she has the flu. She said she would be back next week to clean."

I looked around the untidy room, including papers stacked in the corner from the weekend, and quietly excused myself for a breather. By this time, not only were my cheeks flushed and my heart pounding, but my head throbbed with the beginning of a tension headache.

Juggler? But who was being deceived and cheated? I lay on top of my unmade bed and closed my eyes. We had it all, didn't we? Financially secure, Christian home, three responsible children, two cars, one dog, many vacations, and more. But did we really have it all?

I felt my face as I lay on the bed focusing on the many responsibilities of the day. Flushed skin. Heart pounding. Throbbing head. Fatigue. Stress. Who was being deceived and cheated? Was it me?

The rest of that week of my rebirth, I carefully evaluated everything I did at work and at home. I began to see that there was little time for me to do the things that were important to my well-being and growth. Sure, I was liberated: I could bring home a paycheck like any career person. I could raise responsible children in a loving Christian home like a caring mother. I could teach Sunday school and serve on committees at church like a devoted disciple. And I was also quite talented at being a psychologist, chauffeur, chef, seamstress, and more.

But where was the time for me? Where were those precious moments for reading the Bible, visiting with my family, writing, or making those phone calls to friends I once had? Where was the alertness that was necessary to listen to a nine-year-old's story about playing chase on the playground? Where was the compassion that was needed for my teenage daughter as she entered the ninth grade? And what about my teenage son? Sure he was in high school, but didn't he still need an interested parent to "be there" when he had problems?

Juggler? Cheated? You'd better believe it. At the end of the week that was it! After five years of liberation complete with juggling act, I am thankful that I had the option of deciding to stay home to complete my responsibility of raising a family. I realized that in juggling the many responsibilities I had taken on with a career that I didn't need it the way I thought I had, that the person I was ultimately cheating was myself. My hurried day had been exacting a toll that I hadn't been aware of. I had lost sight of myself.

The Bible teaches us in the great commandment: "'Love the Lord your God with all your heart and with all your soul and with all your strength and with all your mind;' and, 'Love your neighbor as yourself'" (Luke 10:27).

I now realize that I am only one person and I have my limitations, but I am beginning to like that person. Ironically, it was in quitting the "juggling business" rather than in starting it that I discovered myself; I find that I am more loving to my husband, children, and friends. I am taking time to hear that "gentle whisper" as God speaks to me in my daily activities.

And because I am not juggling thoughts about other responsibilities, I am now in tune with the daily needs of my children and husband; I can focus on their problems genuinely. I now see liberation as being able to fully be myself in life without feeling the pressure to add so many different roles outside the home. My priorities are now to fulfill the goal of raising responsible children to adulthood in a Christian home. Period. No demanding second career. No fast-paced days. No racing around trying to stay on a tight schedule.

Yes, I turned in my juggler's card, and I am more fulfilled for doing so. My prayer is that if you have the same need, you will have the same option.

32

The Loving Listener

"Everyone should be quick to listen, slow to speak."

—James 1:19

Isn't it amazing how well we listen to a good friend when we are interested in the subject? What happens when the discussion is between parent and child? Often we tune out the conversation, ignore the child, and use all sorts of body language that causes the speaker to feel we are not interested in his thoughts or opinions.

Did you know your reaction to your child's words determines how much he or she will communicate with you? If you come across as unyielding, then your child may feel that it is useless to talk with you and quit trying. If you listen to the other person's reasoning, try to relate to what he is saying without judging what is being said, and then give replies that are fair and reasonable, you are opening the door to loving communication in your family.

Are you a loving listener? Being an effective listener is essential to establishing meaningful relationships. When feelings and thoughts are poured out and real listening occurs, your child will feel loved and understood. Our own Lord exhibited these same listening skills as He patiently dealt with people and problems each day. In fact, the Bible has much to teach about communication. Remember in John 8:1–11 how Jesus patiently listened to the scribes and Pharisees as they accused the woman of adultery, His kind words to her, and how He solved the problem without harsh punishment? Jesus listened intently to the problem before responding.

Unfortunately, some of us are lazy listeners. When listening to those we love, we often shuffle our feet, yawn excessively, and look here and there, as if to say, "This subject is not interesting."

This non-verbal expression, this body language, can make the difference in whether your listening skills are effective. While you listen, the way you sit or stand, the way you cross your legs, the way you gesture or smile, greatly affect how the other person feels. Posture is closely linked to the mood of the moment. If you seem stiff and rigid, the other person will feel uncomfortable while speaking. If you are too loose and relaxed, too casual, the other person may think you are indifferent to what he is saying. So if your body language is negative and your replies are also negative, your total listening ability could score a zero.

Facial expressions also can enhance or detract from your listening skills. When Jan told her daughter she made the right choice in her prom dress, Karen did not believe her.

"Mom's face told the whole story; I could see in her eyes that she didn't like my choice at all," she later told her best friend.

An affable, responsive face can be a tremendous asset for listening in love. But if you tend to betray your slightest reservation with your eyes, then an honest report of that is the best policy. For your expressions should carry conviction and encourage reassurance as the other person confides in you. If you make eye contact and keep it, you show your sincerity and interest in what the other person is saying.

Besides body stance, posture, and facial expressions, timing is equally important. To be an effective listener, you must know how to read the other person. Does the person appear restless? Is there noise or some other distraction you have to compete with? Be aware of anything that could distract and hinder the communication and result in your misunderstanding the message.

What is involved in becoming a careful listener? Can you really learn to be a loving listener? Let's look at some ways to become a sensitive listener so that the message we communi-

cate to our children is one of compassion and empathy.
- Look directly at your child when talking. While listening, refuse to talk to or look at anyone else, even if just to smile. Each time you look away while listening to your child, the communication is diminished. Each time you pay attention, you are showing the courteous due someone you love.
- Make sure you understand what is being said. Ask your child questions about the subject being discussed. Do not assume anything that is not said. Restate what your child says and ask if that is correct, such as "Did I hear you say that. . . ?" Get all the facts straight before offering an opinion, a suggestion, or a comment.
- Force yourself to keep your mind on the subject being discussed. Don't let your mind wander to the problems at work or needs of the home. Try to identify with your child and what he is telling you. Reflect on your own life. Were you ever in that situation? How did it feel? How did you solve it? Respond to and think about the message your child is expressing in both words and feelings.
- Care enough to be sensitive about what is being said even if it is totally irrelevant to your life. Don't shrug off your child's words and feelings. Empathize. Let your child know of your love and support.
- Accept what your child is telling you. This does not mean that you have to agree; it means you are hearing what is said. This acceptance relays a caring message as you respect your child's feelings and expressions.

Listening skills are critical for making people feel loved, affirmed, and understood. If you seem uninterested when your child communicates with you, he may feel frustrated and quit talking to you. If you really listen, you can have empathy for the situation your child describes.

Are you a sensitive listener? For better communication, tune in to your child, focus on the message you hear, and respond with empathy. Listening to our children is where our efforts at better communication should begin—not end.

33

Teaching Your Child to Cope

"Do not be afraid or discouraged, for the Lord God . . . is with you. He will not fail you or forsake you."

—1 Chronicles 28:20

When my daughter began complaining about stomachaches each day before school, I thought her problem was something she was eating. When the problem persisted, I knew we were dealing with something more serious.

"I believe Ashley is under stress," her pediatrician said after carefully checking her symptoms. "Has she undergone any dramatic changes lately at school or at home?"

Yes, she had undergone change. Our family was new to the city and she was new to her school. For the first time in her life, she was forced to reach out, make new friends, and be the "new kid." This change had overwhelmed Ashley, resulting in the stress-related symptoms.

We don't often think about it, but a child can have just as much difficulty coping with life as an adult. It is a great mistake to think children are unaffected by the crises that their parents experience. In fact, professionals claim that stress is contagious; when parents are undergoing a period of pressure, so will the children.

Stress is the word used to describe the many demands and pressures that all people, even children, experience in daily living. These demands in life require us to change or adapt in some fashion, perhaps physically, perhaps psychologically.

What causes stress in children? Let's look at some common factors that can produce anxiety even in a seemingly calm home environment.

1. Pressure to be successful at an early age. Many parents live vicariously through their children and place tremendous pressure on them to be outstanding athletes, students, or socialites. When this parental pressure is too great, the result is stress.

2. Early exposure to the media. Our children are exposed to violence as soon as they are old enough to watch television. It has been said that one week in front of the television set will give today's child as much exposure to the real world as earlier generations saw in a lifetime.

3. Separation and transition in the family. Divorce, stepparents, moving, death, and general uneasiness all create an anxious child. Children who used to feel secure knowing the family unit was intact now worry about who they will come home to.

4. Economic insecurities. Hard times create more stress in the family, even for children. Children hear parents talk about not being able to pay bills or afford a vacation. They may interpret this to mean there will not be enough money for basics such as food and clothing, and they may become anxious about their future.

5. Social pressures to grow up too fast. Even young children are bombarded with advertisements that encourage behavior and dress that are too sophisticated for their years. Advertisements focus on making everyone "young and beautiful." Children do not have the maturity and wisdom to cope with this early emphasis on sexuality. This creates added stress.

Stress can show itself through a wide variety of physical changes and emotional responses. Stress symptoms vary greatly from one child to the next. Perhaps the most universal sign of childhood stress is a feeling of being pressured or overwhelmed. Parents need to be careful listeners and realize when the symptoms occur.

- Physical complaints—stomachaches, headaches, diarrhea
- Problems with peers or problems at school—a well-behaved child becomes a fighter or a good student begins to fail
- Changes in behavior at home—temper tantrums, unexplained anger

- Regression—behavior that is not age-appropriate
- Sleep patterns—nightmares, too little or too much sleep
- Communication difficulty—a withdrawn child requires much attention or an extrovert becomes withdrawn
- Impatience—the child seems to have a low tolerance for frustration

If you recognize many of these characteristics in your children, chances are good that their level of stress is excessive. If left untreated, stress in your family, especially in your child, can lead to permanent feelings of helplessness and ineffectiveness. Worry and tension that build up in children can cause psychological and physical symptoms that can impair their well-being.

Coping Strategies for Stress

1. Talk with your children about stressful situations they might encounter. Help them recognize such body signals as a hot, flushed face, racing heart, or pains in the stomach, so they will realize when they are anxious. You can point out what might cause these reactions: a bad grade, family conflict, peer problems.

After mentioning each possible cause, talk with your child about his or her reaction. Does he feel physically sick? Does he feel as if no one cares? Does he want to give up some activity or quit some group because of peer problems? At such times your support is crucial to the well-being of your children. Such parent-child communication can prepare them to cope.

2. Give your children comfort and assurance. Children must realize that everyone, even parents, has similar feelings under stress. Parents must be the ones to share this information. When you talk about situations in your own life that make you uncomfortable and share your feelings with your children, they will develop a better self-esteem, accepting their own fears as normal.

3. Brainstorm ways of coping with worries and stressful situations. Suggest ways your child can cope with pressure: breathing deeply, closing the eyes and imagining a peaceful scene (perhaps quoting the Twenty-Third Psalm) or relaxing different parts of the body. Practice methods of relaxation with your child that will enable him to combat stress.

4. Help your child look at personal problems objectively. We all have problems—those we can do something about and those we cannot. Talk to your children about their concerns and needless worries. A divorce in the family is a problem which a child has no control over; on the other hand, a poor grade can be raised with some extra help, or tutoring. An ailing grandparent is out of the child's control, but being overweight may be altered with the help of a caring physician. If your children can begin at a young age to sort the problems they can control from those they can't, they will be the winners in later years as they recognize and eliminate unnecessary worry and stress.

5. Find a support group for your child. Everyone needs someone to talk to—someone who will listen to problems, joys, and concerns. If you are unable to be this person for your child, help him or her to talk to the pastor or a youth counselor. Clubs or church groups might offer support as other children share personal dilemmas and how they are solving them. Trained professionals are ready to guide you in a positive direction.

6. Have your children examine their lives carefully. Make a comprehensive list of all the things that cause them stress. Eliminate or avoid those that are not absolutely necessary. Try to modify the others.

Stress in adults and children becomes magnified when it's not verbalized and shared. You can help your children learn control as they make changes in both their thinking and acting. Most of all, let them know they are never alone; God is with them.

34

Letting Go in Love

"There is a time for everything, and a season for every activity under heaven."

—Ecclesiastes 3:1

When our youngest child was six years old, I watched her walk down the crowded halls to her first-grade classroom. I remember asking the student in the patrol uniform if I could escort her to the class, but he shook his head emphatically. He then quoted the rule in the PTA handbook: "All adults must check into the main office to receive a permission slip to go into a classroom." I could hardly stand it! Here was my "baby" leaving me for almost the entire day, and these patrols had orders to "hold back parents." The irony of the situation as I recall was that young Ashley didn't even hesitate; she approached the new experience in her life with complete confidence.

To watch one's child break away and become independent is painful. How can we release to the cruel world the child who was once so dependent on us?

As the parent-child bond becomes fragile and thin, the relationship develops into one of independence, then interdependence and love.

We really have little choice in the matter of letting go as the child becomes older and begins to make his own decisions. I received a foretaste of this even as I brought my child into the world. I recalled the brief hospital stay with my first child. I wanted so much to hold him, to get to know him (rooming-in with the baby was not yet practiced in this conservative hospital). Instead, I had to accept only those precious, brief moments during feeding time to have my child all to myself.

It occurs to me that even when my child was only minutes old, many other people were necessary to his development, providing nurture and care for him: the night nurse who diligently rocked him during those fussy moments, the elderly volunteer who kept him clean and dry during the day. Even the young pediatrician who registered his vital signs as my baby made his debut became important in his new world.

Even though I was the one who had carried him for nine months, labored for hours to present him to the world, and prepared the perfect environment at home to take him to, I had to begin letting go even then.

It's good to realize that letting go is a part of life; it can come at the most unexpected times: a debilitating illness in the prime of life, the sudden death of a loved one—even the first steps of your baby. By realizing that letting go is inevitable, and accepting it as a reality of life, the pain can be less acute.

Once Brittnye and I were enjoying "sale" shopping at the nearby mall. As we hurried from store to store taking advantage of the bargains, we saw her best friend from school. "Oh, do let Britt come home with us for the afternoon," the girl's mother pled.

"Oh, yes! Please, Mom," said my daughter. Then seeing the disappointment in my eyes of losing her on our special shopping trip, she added, "You wait for me, and we can talk tonight." I never told anyone that I cried that afternoon.

A brilliant young man in our local church recently became critically ill. As death appeared imminent, he began to minister to his grieving family. He told them of the tremendous peace he felt and of the love he had for a living God who offers strength and comfort. The beauty of his personal faith gave strength to those around him.

Letting go often involves caring more for the needs of others than for our own. Brittnye's need to be with her friend, to experience the fantasies and laughs that only two preteens can share, outweighed my motherly need to be with her. As the young man slipped away to be with his Heavenly Father and the intense pain that no medication could relieve was ended, his loved ones felt assured that letting go was a part of loving.

I have realized through my own experience and through observing others in parenting situations that trying to keep children dependent soothes and comforts only the parents. Encouraging a strong dependence on the parent hinders the child in maturing and developing. Allowing my children to participate in extracurricular school activities, soccer teams, or gymnastic classes enables them to grow and develop. I remind myself of this as I drive numerous carpools and patiently wait with other caring mothers.

As a mother I try to weigh each decision I make regarding my child's activities. I ask myself, *Is the letting go at this point appropriate, premature, or overdue?* Sometimes I don't let go because the child is not ready for the activity or because the activity will not aid in building his personality and character. Sometimes I deliberately say no because I want the child to be near me, to fill my own loneliness or insecurity. Then I'm not really caring for the child but for myself. I live with guilt during those times.

As a parent, I must be careful to give the necessary freedom for my child to experience the outside world. The child needs interaction with peers, opportunity to make decisions, and to be in different surroundings. Children who are overprotected may rebel in later years, or they may become too dependent and never develop the ability to make their own decisions.

A friend believed that her child needed her more than peer interaction and kept a firm grip on her young son by selecting only those playmates she felt were acceptable, planning extra activities, limiting his social environment. She made all the decisions for him in those formative years rather than letting her son make friends and decisions on his own.

Now as an adolescent, the boy has found a new freedom, opposite of what his mother dreamed. He is sneaking out of the house at all hours of the night, choosing peers with values unlike his, and defying her positive intentions for him. By not gradually letting go of the child in the beginning, she faced total rebellion when the child grew older.

Caring enough to let go involves letting your children make mistakes—fail—and then opening your arms without saying I told you so when the child comes running home. As you help pick up the pieces, you are enabling him to grow from his failure.

Many parents watch in despair as their young adult children experiment in life-styles that are not Christian. The bond between parent and child is strained to the breaking point. As in the story of the Prodigal Son, the parent waits with loving, caring arms outstretched for the child to come to his senses. Parental love helps to heal the broken young life.

Does letting go become easier as children grow older? Recently I attended the wedding of my youngest sister. Other family weddings had been joyous occasions with laughter and teasing from the family; this wedding, on the other hand, held a peculiar sadness. It marked a dramatic end to a stage of life for my parents. They were no longer directly responsible for rearing children. New doors were opening for them, and a new phase of life was beginning. Letting go of their youngest child and memories of all of the years of being a family under the same roof stirred deep emotions. Accepting the fact that letting go is a part of life can help ease the pain of such an experience.

But as I said, sometimes we have little or no choice in letting go. While our youngest daughter was in the emergency room a few years ago, a team of surgeons told us she must face surgery that night to repair a torn muscle. The doctors would not say the muscle could be fixed or even that the child could withstand the surgery. We had no choice, however; her life was at stake. As we let go and allowed our child to undergo the surgery, we placed our total faith in a God who was using the doctors to heal her. Our positive attitude that we had made the right decision sustained us during the surgery. Today, she is fully recovered.

As I treasure precious moments with my family, I know a day will come when I will no longer be making decisions for them. As they mature, they will choose their own mate, their own career, their own place in the world. As I grow older, I hope that I shall also grow wiser, that I shall grow in grace, so I can in complete trust and faith let them go; this is the goal of Christian parenting. Faith in a loving God who gives strength and guidance enables us to let go in love.

"Here was my 'baby' leaving me for almost the entire day, and these patrols had orders to 'hold back parents.'"

35

What Will They Remember?

"Whatever is in the heart overflows into speech."
—Luke 6:45, *Living Bible*

Have you ever wondered what your children will say about you years from now? Will they remember the time you took to be with them, to teach them, to care for them? Will they hold high the moments you prayed with them, took them to church, and taught their Bible classes? Will the children have memories of family picnics, moments alone with one parent, and laughter at the dinner table?

What we say and how we act toward our children is the strongest influence on their lives. Our thoughts, feelings, and behavior mirror our soul. If we are full of depressing thoughts, doubts, and suspicions regarding our children, then their attitudes toward life become negative. If we are enthusiastic, hopeful, and positive, our parenting skills can be filled with benefits for them. Our actions and words can have a vibrant impression on our children, especially as we train them in the unique manner in which God intended.

As Christian parents, we must hold high the honor and glory of Christ's holy name as we make time to teach our children the ways that lead to life eternal. We must rejoice in the truth that Jesus is alive and base our faith on His resurrection story. And because He is also alive in our hearts, we can rejoice in telling this good news to our children.

How do we teach our children? Teaching our children each day is not difficult! An early morning walk around the block with your eight-year-old becomes the perfect time to talk about life and God's creation. Watching the bright sun rise in the pale sky with your teen affirms the strength of God's work and of your love for your child. Stopping with your preschooler to watch a spider as it awakens in its dew-drenched web shows us hope in our own lives. By being a positive Christian role model each day, we give our children strength to grow up in a secular society.

Having an attitude of anticipation of God in life's experiences can help your child develop a relationship with Him. As you take time to mediate an argument between your children, behold the beauty of a rainbow after a storm, or wipe a tear when feelings are hurt, you can share messages about God.

Teaching your children involves being a living example of what you say. Saying one thing and doing another will only confuse the child. For example, the parent who tells his child it is wrong to lie, then tells his boss he is ill so he can play golf, is teaching a hypocritical faith.

The pages in this book have emphasized the tremendous calling Christian parents have. It is not easy! Telling our children—of all ages—about a living Lord means teaching them about the good and bad that life will offer, then letting them know of the love and new life Jesus can give.

Teaching our children daily involves putting our needs first at times. Remember that you are a person first and a parent second. We cheat our children if we ignore our own personal needs. We have been given the great commandment in the Gospels, "Love your neighbor as yourself" (Mark 12:31). This verse presupposes that we love ourselves. If we are full of personal anger, tensions, and anxieties, perhaps we are not loving ourselves enough. Unless we make time to care for self, we will not be adequate to love and teach our children.

It is not easy to parent in a loving manner every day. But never forget: a family that is secured in God's love through Jesus Christ will be blessed with strength—"a threefold chord is not quickly broken" (Ecclesiastes 4:12).

As you take the challenge of being your child's first teacher and set positive parenting goals for each child with God leading the way, you can begin to experience this ultimate sense of strength, hope, and promise.

Will you teach your children? It is my prayer that someday they will have memories that count, and delight in realizing that all they really needed to know they learned from you—their parents!